AGAINST THE TROIKA

AGAINST THE TROIKA

CRISIS AND AUSTERITY IN THE EUROZONE

HEINER FLASSBECK AND
COSTAS LAPAVITSAS

FOREWORD BY OSKAR LAFONTAINE
PREFACE BY PAUL MASON
AFTERWORD BY
ALBERTO GARZÓN ESPINOSA

VERSO
London • New York

First published by Verso 2015

1 3 5 7 9 10 8 6 4 2

Verso
UK: 6 Meard Street, London W1F 0EG
US: 20 Jay Street, Suite 1010, Brooklyn, NY 11201
www.versobooks.com

Verso is the imprint of New Left Books

ISBN-13: 978-1-78478-313-6 (PB)
eISBN-13: 978-1-78478-315-0 (US)
eISBN-13: 978-1-78478-314-3 (UK)

British Library Cataloguing in Publication Data
A catalogue record for this book is available from the British Library

Library of Congress Cataloging-in-Publication Data
A catalog record for this book is available from the Library of Congress

Typeset in Minion Pro by MJ & N Gavan, Truro, Cornwall

Contents

Foreword

Oskar Lafontaine,
Former president of the Social Democratic Party
and the Die Linke Party in Germany

At the beginning of 2015 Europe finds itself at a critical stage of its development. With the overall economy still in recession, unemployment sky high and a political leadership unable to cope with the complex questions raised by the long-lasting crisis of the European Monetary Union, the idea of a peacefully united European continent is fading away.

For someone like me, who grew up in a small town very close to the French border and was raised in a strong pan-European spirit, the vision of a united Europe, to be reached through the gradual convergence of living standards, the deepening of democracy, and the flowering of a truly European culture, has been a political beacon for many decades.

Today, in face of a neverending crisis of the European institutions and with hardship imposed on millions of guiltless people across Europe, it is deeply worrisome to observe the rise of the ideas of the far right, ideas that we used to consider irreversibly bankrupt. Nationalism, directed explicitly against the idea of a united Europe, is gaining ground in countries of the North as well as of the South.

The reasons for this sad development are described masterfully in this new book by economists Heiner Flassbeck and Costas Lapavitsas, both with extensive international experience in research and policy, while one hails from the North and the other from the South of Europe. They demonstrate with clarity that the mercantilist and deflationary policies pursued by Germany since the beginning of EMU must carry the blame for the great rupture that is currently threatening Europe. Even more disturbing, in the aftermath of the global crisis of 2007–9, a creditor country such as Germany has gained enormous power, but made bad use of it. Austerity and wage cuts, imposed by the creditors on the debtors, have caused a great depression in Greece, while obliterating the notion of a common 'European project'. It would be simply intolerable for democratically elected governments in Paris, Rome or Athens for the direction of their economic policies to be dictated by Berlin.

In light of the unwillingness of Germany to change course and considering the nationalist dangers that attitude is likely to provoke in still more countries of Europe, the warnings of Flassbeck and Lapavitsas should not be ignored. Sometimes it is necessary to take a step back, if progress is to be made. The European Monetary Union, designed to crown European integration, should not become its tombstone. If countries cannot comply with the austerity and other adjustment conditions without endangering democracy and social cohesion, they should be given a way out of the straightjacket of the Monetary Union and be allowed to take their fate in their own hands. If the European Union is unable to assist countries in a truly collegial and associational way, it should proceed to dismantle the unviable Monetary Union, thus creating a fresh basis for a more credible process of integration.

Preface

Paul Mason,
Author and economics editor of Channel 4 News *in the UK*

The OECD won't spell it out themselves, but fifty-year projections by their economists in 2014 carried a dire implication: for the developed world, the best of capitalism is over. Long-term growth rates are likely to be suppressed – by low productivity, high ratios of elderly people to young workers and an overhanding debt problem that, in turn, demands greater wage austerity and inroads into the welfare state.

For the immediate future the crisis has created an oversupply of workers and capital, and an undersupply of profits, wages, inflation and growth. And this changes the macroeconomic game. National economic strategy has, for the whole neoliberal era, been premised on the assumption that the global game was 'win–win' and the best way to play it was through collaboration.

But, in the seventh year of post-Lehman austerity, that is no longer true. Recession has turned into a long stagnation for the developed world; and with each of the BRIC countries now facing a structural crisis, it is time for policy makers to take a long stare at that fifty-year horizon and rethink.

If growth is dwindling, the imperative for any country becomes, first, to secure a fair share of it and, second, if possible more than that.

And that, effectively is what three out of four major players in the world economy have begun to do: America, through its fiscal deficit, bank bailouts and quantitative easing policy, has cornered most of the growth available to the West; and Japan and China are now locked in an undeclared currency war, each using loose monetary policy to maintain growth.

Only Europe refuses to compete. Its national elites, and the supra-national elite around the EU institutions, can only repeat the broken mantras that have led the continent towards stagnation.

The European Central Bank (ECB) has consistently acted late, and conservatively, in the use of monetary policy to mitigate the stagnation crisis. Only in 2012, faced with an existential bond crisis, did it begin to use policy tools unconventionally. Even now, as this book goes to press, it is not clear whether it can bring itself to deliver full quantitative easing.

With fiscal policy, the entire continent is locked in – at Germany's behest – to a damaging and needless austerity: policy-created output gaps at 2 or 3 per cent of GDP even for the healthiest economies will look – to our grandchildren – like madness. We are facing a century of stagnation so we impose stagnation some more to meet rules designed in a previous era.

The barometer of policy dysfunction is now clear: political discontent. The party political systems in Japan, China and even – for all the shouting – America remain intact. But in many European countries there is now a right-wing conservative nationalist opposition with double-digit support: UKIP, the Front National, the Sweden Democrats. In Spain and Greece, almost out of nowhere, there are radical left parties with a serious chance of winning elections.

In the face of mass unemployment and now the political threat from outsider parties, the complacency of the European elite is striking. They were always the embarrassed underachievers within neoliberalism: the EU was the only free market project in the world saddled with a high-cost welfare state and an overt social contract with its workforce. They believed in neoliberalism more than they were allowed to practise it.

So while the US presidency can tough-out one 'fiscal cliff' negotiation after another with Congress, the EU sticks to its own rules, and to a busted ideology, and as a result millions of young people sit at home workless, live with their parents, or occupy their hours with 'bullshit jobs' that pay little and contribute even less.

For conservative parties, whose mass base is the middle class, the financial elite and the now vast army of servants that lives inside the rentier bubble, such political crises are survivable. For the centre left it is different. Complacency has proved suicidal.

The Greek Pasok party would rather self-destruct than protect the worker and middle-class electoral base from austerity. The Spanish PSOE had to watch as, from nowhere, a rival, vibrant leftist party eclipsed it. In Scotland the Labour Party faces near wipeout, after it conducted a last-ditch defence of unity with England, while vast masses of young and working-class people wanted independence on a social justice platform.

This is a pallid, talentless, hyper-cautious generation of social democrats. They can't speak the language of their own traditional support base, the working class, nor of the networked youth who swarmed onto the streets in 2012. And that's because they cannot see an alternative to austerity.

In this book, the authors present one alternative: managed exit from the Euro and a return to nationally sovereign central banks. They argue that political union and a 'transfer union' whereby taxation and spending are pooled, are impossible inside the EU, and that any social justice project must inevitably clash with the European institutions.

For those who, to the contrary, still believe Europe can be reformed to deliver social justice, growth and high-welfare societies, the authors do the valuable service of spelling out what that would take: the defeat not only of the mainstream conservative parties but also of their right-wing, nationalist challengers, and the total transformation of European social democracy in the direction of heterodox, fiscally expansionist economic policy, and the triumph of the as yet untested new left parties.

The years 2015 and 2016 are critical: what happens in Britain, Greece, Spain and ultimately France will determine whether Europe falls apart under the combined pressure of the new right and the unorthodox left. If it survives, then the vast majority of mainstream politicians who want it to are currently wedded to policies that will make that survival synonymous with stagnation, austerity and social disintegration.

Europe's survival as a project to deliver social justice, sustainable and equitable development and democratic values is now under severe threat. The neoliberal elites of Europe are clustered in the modern Versailles – Davos, the yachting ports and the guarded mansions – oblivious.

Those who want a Europe of fiscal expansion, courageous and unorthodox monetary policy, and aggressive competition with the rest of the world for growth, for people, for high-tech capacity need to be able to answer: what if that does not happen? The authors here spell out the logic: exit, breakup and the reconstitution of social justice projects within nation states, or smaller alliances of nation states.

Nobody wants a 'return to the 1930s'; but if – as I suspect – the competitive exit phase from the post-2008 crisis has begun, then the lesson of the 1930s is that the last one out loses. Europe has had seven years to resolve the post-Lehman crisis using the old rules and methods, and has failed. It now has either to unite and compete or face breakup. Its own populations will not stand this combination of economic stagnation and political pallor for much longer.

CHAPTER 1

The Deepening Crisis of the European Monetary Union[1]

The last seven years have been a tumultuous period for Europe and the unrest is far from over. The global crisis that began in 2007 led to a sharp financial shock in 2008–9, which ushered in a recession across the world. Europe – including Germany – was hit hard as credit contracted and international trade shrunk. The real crisis in Europe, however, commenced in 2009–10 as the recession induced a worsening of public finances that triggered off a gigantic crisis in the Eurozone.

During the initial period, the Eurozone crisis was particularly sharp in the periphery (mostly Greece, Portugal, Spain and Ireland) which was effectively shut out of global financial markets and faced deep recession. Greece was the first country to be affected and was eventually to prove the hardest hit. In 2010 many observers considered the unrest to be mainly a crisis of Greece, mostly due to the level of its public debt. Greece certainly has particularly deep problems, discussed in depth in the final chapters of this study. However, five years later, it is undeniable that the deeper aspect of the European turmoil is that of a crisis between Germany and other important core countries. With France and Italy trapped in overvaluation of their effective exchange rates – representing a loss of competitiveness due to German wage dumping – the prospects for the survival of the European Monetary Union and of the European Union as a whole are bleak.

The response of EU authorities to the crisis has cast light on the very nature of the European Union. After an initial period of confusion during which the blame was laid squarely on bad public finances in the periphery (becoming extremely spiteful in the case of Greece), it was realised that the core of the monetary union itself was at risk. Gradually

---

1 Several parts of this book draw on Flassbeck and Lapavitsas, 2013, and on Lapavitsas et al., 2012.

a policy response of 'bailouts' was formulated that took its cue from IMF interventions across the world in previous years as well as from the neoliberal economics that currently dominates thinking within the EU. The response has had five basic components:

> i) Liquidity support was provided to banks by the ECB to prevent banking collapse.
> ii) Emergency loans were provided to peripheral states to prevent default but also to ensure that individual states remained capable of injecting capital into their national banking systems.
> iii) Austerity was imposed on peripheral countries to stabilise public finances and to reduce national debt.
> iv) Deregulation and privatisation were promoted with the aim of reducing wages ('improving competitiveness') and freeing the operations of private capital in the hope that growth would follow.
> v) Harsh rules were embedded in the constitution of the EU to ensure discipline in public finances. Some small steps were also taken towards banking union.

With the passage of time, it has become clear that the EU response has amouanted to the wholesale conservative restructuring of the EMU, and to the consolidation of deeply problematic economic and power relations in Europe. Even so, the fundamental defect of the monetary union, which lies at the root of the Eurozone crisis, namely the divergence of unit labour costs caused in large measure by the German policy of freezing labour costs, has been tackled neither effectively nor equitably. The burden of adjustment has been shifted mostly onto peripheral countries first, and increasingly onto the deficit countries of the core. In 2014, France and Italy, both of which have played by the rules and have lost competitiveness due to Germany's deflationary policy, have thus found themselves in exceptionally difficult circumstances.

The imposition of austerity on the core has never been as severe as in the periphery, although it has been sufficient to weaken aggregate demand and to squeeze incomes, thus affecting economic performance negatively. However, 'austerity light' is incapable of restoring the loss of competitiveness, and therefore both countries have continued to perform poorly and to lose ground relative to Germany. And yet, imposing austerity on the scale of the periphery would be a frightening prospect in both France and Italy since it would induce a deep recession across the Eurozone, not to mention boosting the parties of the extreme Right. In short, the core of the Eurozone is at an impasse of historic proportions, reflecting the failure of the monetary union.[2]

Germany has been strengthened by the Eurozone crisis, since it has emerged as the continent's dominant exporter and provider of money capital. Its political sway over the EU is unprecedented, having eclipsed France. Nevertheless, Germany's currently powerful position is precariously based. The policy of systematically suppressing wage increases might have generated a competitive advantage within the monetary union, since devaluation of currencies is impossible, but it has also resulted in permanently weak domestic demand. Germany has transformed itself into a vast export machine that sucks in demand from across the world, while its domestic economy performs indifferently at best. This is a very slender basis for growth, as has been evident by the weak performance of Germany between 2011 and 2014.

Moreover, the conservative restructuring on the EMU has transformed the monetary union into a mechanism that promotes recession, high unemployment and low growth across Europe. Not least, the transformation of the EMU has had negative implications for both national sovereignty and democracy across Europe. Germany has come to dominate the EU, but current policies and institutional structures have destroyed the spirit of 'united Europe' and raised the social and political tensions in several countries. The union is probably weaker than at any other time in its history.

---

2   For an analysis of the causes of the Eurozone crisis and the range of policy options available when the crisis burst out, see Lapavitsas, et al., 2012. For further discussion of the causes of the crisis, an analysis of the catastrophic policies actually adopted by the EU, and the gradual shift of the crisis toward the core of the Eurozone, see Flassbeck and Lapavitsas, 2013.

CHAPTER 2

The Theoretical Rationale of a Monetary Union

There is little doubt at the beginning of 2015 that the crisis of the EMU has not gone away. Despite some signs of relief, such as falling interest rate spreads relative to German Bunds and a bottoming out of the steep recession of the preceding period, the ability of EMU to survive this crisis with an unchanged number of participants is far from being warranted. Unorthodox measures by the European Central Bank, in particular its promise to do 'whatever it takes' to stabilise the currency system in 2012, have calmed the financial markets and provided space for economic policy to act in a stabilising way.

However, the majority of the political players, and among them the most important ones in the large countries of the Eurozone, especially those with surpluses, are still struggling to find adequate answers to the challenges raised by the sudden appearance of huge splits and divergences in a formerly homogeneous currency system. The political discourse is dominated by the attempt to convince the deficit countries to follow the path laid down by the surplus countries. Neither the obvious fallacy of composition in policy making (i.e., that all countries taken together could replicate what a single country might be able to do), nor the threat of forcing the whole Eurozone into deflation has yet permeated through the thick layers of political prejudice that have prevented a reasonable and constructive political debate among member states since the beginning of the crisis.

Nevertheless, at the level of the European institutions, awareness appears to be mounting that radical changes are needed to make the system more resilient. And even beyond the traditional obsession with fiscal deficits and government debt, the adoption of an early warning mechanism that could deal with the core of the trouble has proceeded quite quickly. The introduction of the Macroeconomic Imbalance

Procedure (MIP), aimed at dealing with existing and future current account balances and guiding member states towards more balanced trade, has marked some progress towards understanding that a currency union requires, above all, coordination of price and wage evolution.

⊠. The Case for Monetary Cooperation

It has been argued elsewhere that monetary union in Europe was not necessarily a bad idea from the outset.[1] Its likely failure in the future would reflect, first, a lack of sound economic reasoning behind the politically motivated decision to accelerate European integration and, second, the emergence of strong economic and social interests within core countries – primarily Germany – which have hardened the disastrous path of the EMU.

The launching of EMU could be considered as the final step on the way towards lasting exchange rate stability after a long period during which the members of the European Monetary System (EMS) had attempted to operate systems of fixed but managed exchange rates. After the breakdown of Bretton Woods in 1971–3, many smaller countries across the world quite sensibly refused to adopt a system of fully flexible (market determined) exchange rates. For smaller countries in Europe, monetary cooperation has been an important way of avoiding falling victim to the vagaries of the financial markets, typically followed by the harsh 'conditionality' imposed as part of a 'rescue' delivered by the international organisations of the Washington Consensus. Most European countries, in particular the smaller ones, understood quickly that monetary independence would not necessarily be to their advantage. They recognised that for small open economies tying one's hands could be an optimal solution in monetary affairs.

In the presence of extremely volatile exchange rates, small open economies do not have monetary autonomy, because their monetary authorities are obliged to respond to the pressures of currency markets. The formal autonomy of a central bank (i.e., no obligation to intervene) lacks a material basis.[2] Obviously, countries under this

---

1 See Flassbeck and Lapavitsas, 2013.

2 Even so, the bulk of the academic literature still relies in one way or another on the Optimum Currency Area (OCA) theory, or on the so-called 'policy trilemma' of open economies, i.e., their inability to achieve at once

Optimum Currency Areas

Academic attempts since the 1960s to define the criteria for Optimum Currency Areas (OCA) have been in vain. The case that OCA theories generally make is valid only if there is a viable alternative to fixing exchange rates for small open economies in the form of free floating. But in reality there is no such alternative. Monetary autonomy, i.e., the promise of free floating, is a theoretical fiction, something that has been well understood by many countries in Europe long before the Euro was invented. Market-determined exchange rates tend to over- and undershoot the fair – or equilibrium – values, as determined by purchasing power parity (PPP) or by uncovered interest parity (UIP). Even worse, market-determined exchange rates often move in the wrong direction for extended periods of time as a result of currency speculation, the so-called 'carry trade'. [1] Countries with relatively high rates of inflation and, concomitantly, relatively high interest rates tend to be swamped by inflows of short-term funds which drive up the exchange rate of their currencies in real terms. This destroys both absolute and comparative advantage in international trade and distorts the production structure between tradable and non-tradable goods. Under these circumstances, formal monetary autonomy becomes an empty shell.

---

[1] See UNCTAD, Trade and Development Report 2010.

constraint would have to cooperate with other countries to achieve a degree of exchange rate stability sufficient to protect their competitiveness and to allow for balanced trade relations. From the perspective of these countries the valuation of currencies is too important to be left to the market.

In the absence of cooperation, conflict would be unavoidable, as a change in one country's exchange rate would always affect another country. For n countries in the world as a whole there would be $n-1$ exchange rates. Consequently, the crucial question would be not about the need for international monetary cooperation, which is obvious, but about viable forms of cooperation. European monetary cooperation evolved in rather small steps over a period of thirty years before culminating in the full monetary union in 1999.

---

stability of the exchange rate, freedom of capital flows and monetary autonomy. In a system of floating rates the trilemma is a dilemma.

All traditional forms of international monetary cooperation – other than a full monetary union – require that one of the member countries would serve as an anchor for the system. Other countries would adjust their policies in relation to the anchor country. Successful monetary cooperation aimed at enlarging the room of manoeuvre for economic policy in a region as a whole would have to include at least one country that could act as lender of last resort in times of crisis. This need arises due to the asymmetry in the relations between countries whose currencies are under threat of depreciation and those whose currencies are under pressure to appreciate. Countries trying to avoid currency depreciation (or to stop depreciation at a certain point) have to intervene in the currency market. This means their central banks have to increase demand for their own money by selling international reserves. Since such reserves are always limited, countries that are threatened by depreciation are vulnerable to speculative attacks on their currency. The only way to fend off such an attack would be cooperation with the 'other side', i.e., with countries that have appreciating currencies.

In Europe, Germany was the obvious candidate to become the anchor in regional monetary cooperation. Over several decades Germany has been the champion of price stability, as witnessed, in particular, by the smooth absorption of the inflationary consequences of the two oil price shocks. As a result of low inflation, the German currency never came under depreciation pressure but always tended to be on the appreciation side. Hence, Germany assumed the role of the European monetary anchor for good reasons.

Some smaller countries were able to copy the German inflation performance and to maintain exchange rate stability without a loss of overall competitiveness. Austria was the most impressive case in this respect. Most of the larger European economies, however, time and again had to accept depreciation against the German currency to compensate for domestic inflationary bouts. This was especially true for France and Italy, at least up to the mid-1980s. Anchoring proved to be successful in terms of the effective pressure on domestic inflation as long as exchange rate adjustments remained an option to restore unsustainable competitive positions among countries.

During the period of the EMS that preceded EMU and lasted roughly from 1980 to the end of the century, fixed exchange rates in Europe were seen as a tool to foster the completion of the single European market. In addition, Germany, with its stable economic performance and a strongly dogmatic stance on inflation, was increasingly seen as a role model for other countries. The political will to adhere to economic policies and a monetary model similar to that pursued by Germany shaped the European debate on monetary policy and exchange rates to a very large extent.

Monetary Union and Its Sequential Logic

The crucial economic argument for crowning regional monetary cooperation with a monetary union has never been adequately appreciated. In a multi-currency system with one currency acting as anchor, mutual agreement on economic policy and monetary policy would not be tantamount to an optimal solution for all member states. The anchor country's policy, even if it were optimal for the conditions prevailing in that country itself, would not necessarily be optimal policy for the group as a whole. That would still hold even if there was consensus regarding the inflation target among the countries participating in the area of fixed exchange rates.

Indeed, this was the main problem of the Bretton Woods system during the 1950s and 1960s, when the US Dollar served as the anchor currency of the global exchange rate system with fixed but adjustable rates. Decision-making by the US Federal Reserve System (then the de facto global central bank) typically took into account only the economic conditions of the United States, rather than the requirements of the system as a whole.

Similarly, Germany accepted its role as the anchor of the European Monetary System, but decision-making on monetary policy, including the setting of interest rates, was never conducted in view of the requirements of the system as a whole. This policy stance by Germany was clearly inadequate. Thus, the only adequate long-term policy option for regional monetary stability was to form a monetary union. Only in a genuinely multilateral monetary system would all countries be able fully to participate in the decision-making process on monetary policy that would take into account the economic conditions of the whole area. Nothing short of a monetary union could help avoid systemic mismanagement of monetary policy in a region where countries would agree to stabilise both the internal and the external value of money. Thus, in Europe the step to create the EMU was much more than merely an attempt by the French government to prevent German political domination, as has often been claimed. Rather, it was fully justified from an economic point of view, given that Germany as the anchor of the EMS could not create the conditions for a truly European monetary policy.

For very small and extremely open economies, the anchor approach could work for quite some time, if the anchor country's economic policy treated the small satellites in the system with benign neglect. But for any larger group of countries and for countries of similar size and economic power, the anchor approach could only be considered as a transitional stage on the way to a full monetary union. The only way to ensure a consistent monetary policy for the group as a whole would be to form a common central bank. It is important to stress, however, that the transitional phase may last very long. From the first steps towards monetary cooperation to creating the EMU, it took Europe thirty years to accomplish that logical and consequent idea.

From a global perspective, the move towards monetary union supported by a strong political will to coordinate policies provided Europe with an enormous degree of independence vis-à-vis the rest of the world, the international financial markets and international financial organisations. With an anchor strong and stable enough to weather even big international storms the group was able to fend off strong external shocks. No single country of the EMU had to call upon the IMF to overcome problems of exchange rate misalignment and/or lack of international liquidity before the 2010 crisis broke out.

One final point to mention is that command over world money is a measure of international political power which, in the case of the Euro and due to its creditor position, means primarily German power. It ought to be stressed that the EMU was not originally a plan to promote German ascendancy, but rather a formal, treaty-based alliance establishing rights and obligations for member states, and relying strongly on the ideology of Europeanism. Nonetheless, for reasons that are made clear below, the Euro has rebounded strongly in favour of Germany which – after the global financial crisis – has emerged as the country able to set economic and social policy across Europe as it is the main creditor. Yet, in view of the coming clash between debtors and creditors inside the Euro area, Germany's pre-eminence remains extremely fragile.

⊠. THE CORE MONETARY PRINCIPLES OF THE EMU

A monetary union is first and foremost a union of countries willing to give up their own national currency for the purpose of creating a common currency. Giving up a national currency implies waiving the right of the national authorities to issue coins and notes and in this way to deploy national money (fiat money). Any decision with respect to issuing money would be delegated to a supranational institution. The decision-making organs of that institution would be designed to reflect the composition of the membership, but no single country would have a majority influence. National central banks still exist within the EMU, but the power to determine monetary policy and all related decisions has been transferred exclusively to the ECB and its Executive Board.

Entering a monetary union also implies giving up national inflation targets and agreeing on a common inflation target for the union as a whole. The Deutsche Bundesbank, the anchor of the EMS and the role model for the ECB, had established monetarism, or the so-called Quantity Theory of Money, as the leading monetary doctrine in the years prior to the EMU. For a monetary union, monetarism would hold that the common central bank would be able to contain inflation across the entire union by steering the money supply and, moreover, that inflation differentials among the member countries would not occur. On this theoretical basis, the control exercised by the ECB over the money supply was deemed sufficient to hold the actual inflation rate of the EMU close to the target set by the ECB.

Even from this questionable theoretical perspective, public budget deficits, which proved to be the most hotly contested topic in the political debate, are not supposed to influence the inflation performance of the union, for there is no systematic relationship between the size of budget deficits and the rate of inflation. For monetarists, no matter how large was the budget deficit of a country, monetary policy could always attain its inflation target by strictly adhering to 'objective' rules governing the expansion of the money supply.

Monetarist theory has been based on weak empirical evidence from the very beginning. Since the 1930s the monetarist dogma has mainly relied on a kind of *post hoc ergo propter hoc* fallacy. Monetarists have typically insisted that, without more money, an inflationary acceleration would not be possible. It is, of course, true that, without an expanding money supply, an inflationary acceleration would be impossible, but it does not at all follow that any monetary expansion would lead to an inflationary acceleration, i.e., monetary expansion is a *necessary* but not a *sufficient* condition for inflationary acceleration. To put it plainly, while more money would be necessary to inflate the economy, it would be by no means sufficient to expand the money supply to inflate the economy.

At the beginning of the 1990s, this key issue of monetary policy, i.e., the capacity of the common central bank to control inflation, was not subject to much critical analysis within the EMU. Notwithstanding some controversy about the necessary degree of independence of the central bank, the overwhelming weight of opinion agreed that control over the monetary supply would be sufficient to control inflation. In this way, price instability could be avoided and the the ECB would be able to replicate what was considered the splendid performance of the Bundesbank during the preceding twenty years.

With the passage of time, however, the intellectual debate gave the cold shoulder to monetarism and adopted a fresh approach to central banking, in many ways influenced by the achievements of the US Federal Reserve System under its chairman Alan Greenspan. This was not without influence on the ECB, which has from the start been a much more open and multicultural institution than the Bundesbank. Given the failure to find convincing evidence of a strong relationship between prices and the traditional money supply aggregates, the ECB gradually deviated from the doctrine of the Bundesbank (the so-called monetary pillar) and turned towards an approach in which the central bank explicitly acts by setting the short-term interest rate in light of its judgement about macroeconomic developments.

Although this approach is more amenable to testing by using methods that go beyond the traditional money supply channel, its impact was blocked by other neoliberal doctrines that proved far too strong to be rejected even in the light of clear evidence. Both the ECB and the European Commission have been dominated by neoliberal thinking during the period that led to the outbreak of the crisis in 2008. It is mainly for this reason that the ECB, as well as the other institutions founded to govern and to protect EMU, have essentially failed in the first decade. The governing institutions of the EMU began to rise from their intellectual slumber only after the global financial crisis of 2007–9 gave international investors a major jolt concerning the ability of peripheral Eurozone members to pay back the debt they had accumulated during the first ten years of EMU.

⊠. Wage Flexibility and Its Consequences

The clearest evidence regarding the dominant role of neoliberal thinking within the institutions of the EU has been offered by labour market

theory, considered to be one of the main doctrinal pillars of the functioning of the common market and the EU as a whole. The so-called
Lisbon Process and a plethora of decisions taken by the European
Council demonstrate the adherence to neoliberal thinking at the top of
EMU. 'Labour market flexibility' and 'improved competitiveness' have
been (and within many circles still are) the mantras guiding the creation of the common market and the attempt to accelerate growth and
job creation.

It ought to be stressed that there is little empirical evidence for
the theoretical belief that flexible labour markets would automatically provide jobs for all those who are willing to work. The absence of
relevant evidence on this issue is as pronounced as for the other fundamental belief in the importance of controlling the money supply and
guaranteeing the independence of central banks to ensure price stability. Indeed, had some different but striking evidence been taken into
account, it would have been possible to prevent both the EMU and the
EU from falling victim to the financial markets and from entering the
current impasse. The most important piece of evidence is the high and
stable correlation between the growth rate of unit labour costs (ULC)
and the inflation rate.

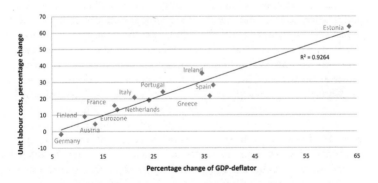

Fig. 1: ULC[1] growth rates and inflation for EMU (1999–2007)[2]

Notes:

1 ULC defined as gross income per capita in ECU/Euro of dependent employees
divided by real GDP per total employed persons

2 For enlarged version of each of the figures, click the hyperlinked title text

Source: AMECO database (as per Nov 12); own calculations

Unit labour costs appear to be the crucial determinant of overall price movements in national economies as well as for groups of economies. Figure 1 demonstrates this simple fact, which ought to be at the core of all macroeconomic reasoning but is widely ignored, usually for ideological reasons.

The cost of labour is the most important component of the total cost of production for the economy as a whole because – in vertically integrated production processes – labour produces final consumer goods as well as intermediate and capital goods. Unit labour costs are the perfect instrument to forecast and control inflation, especially in view of potentially strong political influence that could be exercised on wage setting and wage policy more generally. Specifically, for inflation to hit its chosen target, it would be necessary for nominal wage growth to be in line with national productivity growth plus the inflation target. Astonishingly, the doctrinaire neoliberal approach adopted by the leading institutions of the EU led to profound indifference regarding the evolution of wages and ULC over time.

If the strong correlation between ULC and inflation was acknowledged and placed at the heart of macroeconomic analysis, it would become clear that the main requirement for a successful monetary union would not be control over monetary affairs but rather the management of incomes and nominal wages. To be specific, the common inflation target for EMU was defined by the ECB as a rate close to 2 percent. This implied that the *golden rule* for wage growth in each economy would be the sum of the national growth of productivity plus 2 percent. By this token, large inflation discrepancies leading to competitiveness discrepancies across member countries would not occur.

There is a huge body of evidence showing that a system of fixed exchange rates could function properly only if there were wage adjustments sufficient to compensate for the loss of exchange rate flexibility.[3] Equivalently, it has been very widely observed in systems of fixed but adjustable exchange rates that differences between domestic and international cost levels have to be corrected by changing the external value of the domestic currency (depreciation or appreciation). By this token, in a currency union the necessary adjustment of wages and prices for each member country would play an even more important role than in a system of fixed exchange rates since there would be no option of

---

3   See Flassbeck, 2001.

changing the exchange rate, as in the Bretton Woods system and the EMS.

⊠. Real Wage Growth Determines Domestic Demand

A wage path determined by the golden rule described above would have the additional merit of stabilising domestic demand in all EMU member states. Real wage growth is the most important determinant of domestic consumption growth, therefore systematic adjustment of nominal wages at a rate equivalent to national productivity growth plus the inflation target would stabilise domestic demand in each country, and thus demand across the union as a whole.

To eliminate the impact of unexpected and unforeseeable cyclical changes in productivity it would be preferable to adjust nominal wages to the trend growth of productivity (say, average growth of productivity over the last five years). By taking into account the inflation *target* (rather than the actual rate of inflation) it would be possible to stabilise wage and demand growth. The reason is that short-term and one-off price shocks (for instance, sharp increases in the price of oil or other essential primary commodities) would be prevented from having a lasting inflationary impact. If, in contrast, such shocks were actually reflected in the adjustment of wages – as has been the case in backward-looking indexation mechanisms, such as the *scala mobile* in Italy in the 1970s – the rise in nominal wages would cause a rise in both ULC and the inflation rate, and would eventually command monetary tightening, i.e., the raising of interest rates, which would discourage real investment.

If wage adjustments systematically followed the golden rule, the national economies within the EMU – but also the union as a whole – would move along a stable path, led by generally stable growth of private consumption based on stable increases in incomes expected by households (at least as long as productivity growth was on a positive growth trajectory). Under these circumstances, external trade would also be balanced, because the movement of ULC in tandem with the inflation target in all countries – irrespective of their national productivity paths – would imply stability of the real exchange rate, which is the most comprehensive measure of competitiveness.

It is apparent that stable growth of real wages in line with productivity growth would be in sharp contrast to the proposition that wages should be super-flexible and readily adjustable, as is envisaged by the neoclassical labour market doctrine. According to the latter, high and rising unemployment ('idiosyncratic shocks') would be impossible to cure unless wages were flexible enough to lag behind productivity for extended periods of time. Once again, however, this neoliberal proposition is based neither on evidence nor on logic: with stable growth of domestic income (assured by the chosen adjustment path of real wages) and in the absence of external shocks that would be due to a fall in competitiveness, there would be no idiosyncratic shocks and no need at all to cut real wages.

Indeed, there are severe dangers to overly flexible labour markets. Deflationary traps are usually created by sharply rising unemployment for reasons that are unrelated to labour market developments, such as excessive increases in real wages. High unemployment as the result of a financial crisis, for example, would lead to downward pressure on wages and aggregate incomes, even if wages and incomes were depressed already before the occurrence of the crisis. The combination of high unemployment arising for such reasons together with workers trying to 'price themselves flexibly back into the markets' and thus accepting lower wages would create a perfect storm for economic policy. And this is exactly what happened after the global financial crisis in 2008/2009.

With rising unemployment and renewed pressure on wages, consumer spending did not recover in the way seen in former recessions. In the USA and Europe, the restriction of aggregate demand caused by declining income expectations of households suffering from high levels of unemployment has dramatically prolonged the recession or stagnation. With monetary policy restricted by the lower bound of zero for interest rates, fiscal policy is needed to implement a huge stimulation programme to overcome the decline in aggregate demand in such a precarious situation. Indeed, a large part of the tendency to deflation in contemporary capitalism is the result of a dysfunctional labour market in which unemployment could rise sharply without wages being 'too high'. The lesson is that, for a consistent critical approach to economics, it is necessary to discard both the monetarist theory of inflation and the neoclassical theory of the labour market completely.

The conservative way of getting round the brutal logic of destabilising labour markets would be to hope for improved competitiveness of the economy as a whole and thus for more exports (or fewer imports). Indeed, a solution would seem to be found if a wage cut stimulated foreign demand by more than it depressed domestic demand. These conditions appear to hold for a paradoxical case such as Ireland. Given the country's export share in GDP of more than 100 percent, the positive effect of wage cuts on the current account has balanced out the negative effect on domestic demand. However, Ireland is an exception and hardly relevant to normal economies, or to large groups of countries.

☒. REAL OR NOMINAL CONVERGENCE?

It is frequently argued that countries with very different levels of wealth should not form a monetary union. Poorer countries are assumed to be incapable of competing with richer nations, and are advised to abstain from entering into a race for competitiveness. This argument, however, is not convincing.

The main analytical point in this connection is that, in any country, all groups of agents have to respect a budget restriction in making claims on the income produced in that country: no country can consume more than it produces in the long term. This is why, in a normally functioning economy, the claims of one group, including workers, are balanced out against the claims of other groups at a given level of total income. In an economy in which this balancing does not work, there would be a conflict over income distribution that would result in inflationary bouts and even spirals. If such an outcome was, however, avoided, the level of wages and profits would reflect exactly the level of wealth in that economy, and the wage level would reflect national productivity. Thus, low wages in the poorer countries would reflect low productivity and the opposite for rich countries.

The point here is that the level of nominal unit labour costs would be the same in a poor and in a rich country, provided that in both countries a major conflict about income distribution and inflation could be avoided. Consequently, there would be no risk of large trade imbalances as a result of different levels of wealth as long as some minimum requirements regarding the structure of trade and the structure of products available to both countries would be met, meaning primarily an overlapping structure of goods produced in both countries. This was clearly the case for European countries, which had open trade relations long before entering the monetary union.

Overall, there is no reason why it should not be possible for poor as well as for rich countries to manage the ULC growth in the economy as a whole in such a way that it would be in line with a commonly agreed inflation target. This can be easily demonstrated for France and Germany as in Figure 2 below. Both countries had exactly the same starting point in terms of absolute productivity and nominal wages. However, over time, nominal wages and (in this case, nominal productivity) grew more in France and propelled the country into major difficulties compared to Germany, although French wages have followed a reasonable growth path never violating the golden rule for ULC growth in the monetary union.

The logic of a monetary union built along the lines of EMU demands that member countries must strictly accept the joint target for inflation and to preserve external equilibrium by adjusting wages to national productivity accordingly. For each country, that means strict adjustment to its *own* productivity path and its *own* economic potential. Countries 'living above their means' are as problematic as countries 'living below their means'. The requirement to live 'according to its means' is as pressing as the requirement to commit to free trade for a country that enters a currency union. For, any measures to protect home-made products by imposing barriers on imports or by subsidising exports are strictly forbidden in a common market. In short, if there was no requirement to avoid 'devaluation' of the real exchange rate by undercutting the inflation target through wage 'moderation', the entire body of rules and regulations surrounding a monetary union would be totally useless.

Germany

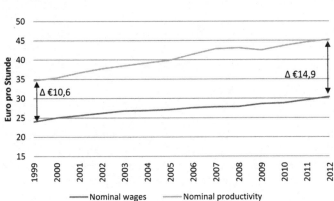

Nominal wages ——— Nominal productivity

France

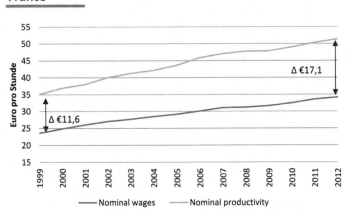

Nominal wages ——— Nominal productivity

Fig. 2: Nominal wages[1] and nominal productivity[2]

Notes:
1 Defined as total nominal compensation of dependent employees divided by working hours of dependent employees times number of dependent employees
2 Defined as nominal GDP divided by working hours of total employed persons times number of employed persons
2012 values for working hours of total employees and dependent employees projected based on data from Destatis and AMECO
Sources: AMECO database (as per November 2012); Eurostat; own calculations

CHAPTER 3

Germany as the Source of the Eurozone Crisis

⊠. POLITICAL PRESSURE TO LOWER WAGES IN GERMANY...

The preparations for EMU were deeply flawed because, instead of discussing the implications of a monetary union in detail and creating the institutions necessary to run such a union successfully, political debate and decision-making in the years up to 1997 – by which time the criteria for entry had to be fulfilled – actually focused on fiscal policy. Particular emphasis was laid on limiting public sector deficits to 3 percent of GDP, whereas the need to avoid inflation differentials and guaranteeing the ability of member states to stick to the common inflation target over time were regarded as much less important issues for the smooth functioning of EMU. Germany, with its absolute intolerance of inflation exceeding 2 percent and its dogmatic monetarist tradition, silenced any other view on inflation.

There is little doubt that the EMU obsession with fiscal targets is the direct result of the struggle between governments and markets that has dominated much of the ideological debate in the thirty years following the end of the Bretton Woods regime. Yet, there is no direct relationship between fiscal budgets and the inflation target (either empirical or theoretical) and any plausible indirect links would be very weak indeed. For neither the current budget deficit nor the size of the public debt has an impact on the inflationary performance of an economy. If any link could be thought of, it would be that (in line with an ancient prejudice) a highly indebted government could perhaps use inflation as a tool to reduce the real value of its debt. However, Japan during the last twenty-five years demonstrates that none of this holds in contemporary capitalism. With a public debt equivalent to 250 percent of GDP, Japan has the highest level of public debt of all industrialised countries. And yet, despite continuous efforts, the country has not been able to get out of a deflationary trap. Japanese policy makers might dream of generating a sustainable level of inflation, but their persistent nightmare is deflation.

In the heated debate that took place in Germany about the dangers of inflationary acceleration as EMU was approached, wages or nominal unit labour costs were hardly ever mentioned. Labour costs were considered to reflect the market price for labour. The 'flexibility doctrine' was the broadly accepted view in politics as well as in economics.[1] Consequently, in view of the monetary union commencing in 1999, Germany, the biggest country in the EU and the bastion of stability for several decades, decided to try out a new way of combating its high level of unemployment. In short, the government, together with the employers, started to put political pressure on labour unions in an attempt to restrict the growth of both nominal and real wages.

It ought to be stressed that Germany's vigorous attempt to tackle its persistently high unemployment rate by making its labour market more flexible was not aimed at gaining an advantage within the EMU. Rather, it was grounded in the neoliberal conviction that lower wages would result in more labour-intensive production processes across the economy. Once work-time reduction schemes had failed to deliver the expected result of reducing unemployment, labour union leaders agreed in a tripartite agreement in 1999 to abandon the formula that had hitherto been used to determine wage growth. The formula had ensured equal participation of workers in the gains from productivity growth (the golden rule mentioned above); instead, the unions agreed to 'reserve productivity growth for employment'.[2]

This agreement also implied that there would be a fundamental break with the German tradition of sticking to a low and stable rate of inflation. Historically, Germany had been characterised by moderate wage increases, which ensured that real wages (nominal wages adjusted for inflation) would rise in line with productivity (GDP divided by the number of hours worked). In other words unit labour costs (nominal wages divided by GDP) would generally rise in line with an inflation target of roughly 2 percent. However, as monetarism became the widely accepted doctrine to tackle inflation on the approach to EMU, the new arrangement clearly meant even lower inflation, and its deflationary aspect was not even thought of.

---

1   The 'doctrine' was clearly laid out in OECD, 1994.
2   See Flassbeck, 1997; and Flassbeck and Spiecker, 2005.

⊠. ...Results in a Huge Gap in Competitiveness inside the EMU

The novel German approach to the labour market coincided with the formal introduction of the monetary union, and consequently led to huge divergences in nominal unit labour costs among the members of EMU. The main cause of these divergences was the simple fact that German nominal unit labour costs, the most important determinant of prices and competitiveness, have remained essentially flat since the start of the EMU, as is shown in Figure 3. In contrast, most countries in southern Europe had nominal wage growth that exceeded national productivity growth plus the commonly agreed inflation target of 2 percent by a small but rather stable margin. France was the only country exactly to meet the target for nominal wage growth. French wages rose in line with national productivity performance plus the ECB's inflation target of a rate close to 2 percent:

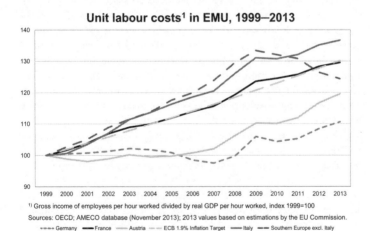

Unit labour costs¹ in EMU, 1999–2013

¹⁾ Gross income of employees per hour worked divided by real GDP per hour worked, index 1999=100

Sources: OECD; AMECO database (November 2013); 2013 values based on estimations by the EU Commission.

━ ━ Germany ━━ France ⎯⎯ Austria ⎯⎯ ECB 1.9% Inflation Target ━━ Italy ━ ━ Southern Europe excl. Italy

Fig. 3: ULC¹ divergence Germany and rest of EMU² (1999 = 100)

Notes:
1 ULC defined as gross income per capita in ECU/Euro of dependent employees divided by real GDP per total employed persons
2 EMU of 11 countries excluding Germany: Belgium, Finland, France, Greece, Ireland, Italy, Luxembourg, Netherlands, Austria, Portugal, Spain
Sources: AMECO database; own calculations

Even though the annual divergence among the increases in ULC was relatively small, the dynamics of such a 'small' annual divergence are able to yield dramatically large gaps over time. At the end of the first decade of EMU the cost and price gap between Germany and southern Europe amounted to some 25 percent, and that between Germany and France to 15 percent. In other words, Germany's real exchange rate had depreciated quite significantly, even though national currencies no longer existed within the EMU. The divergence in the growth of unit labour costs was naturally reflected in equivalent price divergences. Thus, the EMU as a whole achieved the inflation target of 2 percent almost perfectly, but national differences of inflation within the union were remarkable. Once again, France was by far the best performer since it succeeded in aligning its inflation rate perfectly to the EMU target. However, Germany systematically undershot the target and countries in southern Europe systematically overshot it by margins large enough to create huge gaps in competitiveness.

The cumulative gaps have meant huge absolute advantages (and thus disadvantages) in international trade for the countries of the EMU. There is little doubt about the main culprits and the extent of misbehaviour in view of the fact that the ECB's target of nearly 2 percent annual inflation would only be compatible over time with a 2 percent annual increase in nominal unit labour costs. Greece, for instance, was generally delinquent because annual ULC growth was roughly 2.7 percent. But its violation of the rule was much less severe than that by Germany whose annual rate of ULC growth was just 0.4 percent. It is even more paradoxical that Germany had explicitly agreed to the ECB target of close to 2 percent because that had been its own inflation target prior to EMU. Germany was destined clearly to violate the ECB target given that its government and employers had begun to apply enormous downward pressure on wages, aiming at a different capital/labour ratio with the result of improving the country's international competitiveness.

It is undeniable that the real depreciation that has occurred in Germany has had an enormous impact on trade flows. With German unit labour costs undercutting those in the other countries by a rising margin, German exports flourished, while imports slowed down. Countries in southern Europe, but also France and Italy, began to register widening trade and current account deficits and suffered huge losses of their international market shares. Germany, on the other hand, was able to preserve its share despite mounting global competition from China and other emerging markets. In a nutshell, Germany has operated a policy of 'beggar-thy-neighbour' but only after 'beggaring its own people' by essentially freezing wages.[3] This is the secret of German success during the last fifteen years.

While trade within Europe had been rather balanced at the inception of the currency union and for many years before that, the EMU marked the beginning of a period of quickly growing imbalances. Even after the shock of the financial crisis and its devastating effects on global trade that are clearly visible in the German balance, the underlying trend has continued unchanged. Germany's current account has continued to rise after 2010 and even reached a new record high in 2013 (2014 will also see a current account surplus in the order of 200 billion euros or a number of close to 7 percent of GDP). While the surpluses relative to the members of the Eurozone culminated in 2007 the surplus relative to the rest of the world increased quickly after the financial crisis.

It is obvious that immediately after the Eurozone crisis had erupted and the economies of stricken countries had begun to falter, German exporters reoriented their efforts towards the rest of the world and achieved similar surpluses in those markets – still protected by the euro. With a huge accumulated margin of competitiveness in their favour and protected by the relatively low Euro exchange rate (with the exception of a few months in 2014) they could easily gain, again at the expense of other Euro members, market shares in the rest of the world. Chinese demand for automobiles in particular was the most important reason for the surge in exports.

Empirical studies sometimes fail to find evidence for an influence of prices or unit labour costs on trade flows and the current account balance.[4] This is typically due to misspecification of the study or to the uncritical use of country samples and time periods. If, for example, a study also included very small and highly specialised countries, such as Ireland or Cyprus, or poor transitional economies, such as the Baltics, the results are likely to be problematic. The production structure of these countries could not be reasonably compared to countries such as France and Germany with their highly diversified industrial base. Strong objections could also be raised against including in the

---

3 See Lapavitsas, et al., 2012, pt. I.
4 See, for instance, Gabrisch, et al., 2014.

sample a country such as the Netherlands, which has engaged in the German kind of 'beggar-thy-neighbour' policies long before Germany, and was thus able to defend its current account surplus despite its unit labour cost rising more than in Germany since the beginning of EMU.

Moreover, when choosing the period of empirical analysis, it has to be taken into account that the deep recession in the deficit countries of the EMU following the financial crisis of 2008 has naturally tended to reduce the observed deficits through huge income effects that temporarily overlaid the price effects. But it is unlikely that recovery would take place in those countries without a fundamental improvement in competitiveness. The eventual revival of domestic demand, moreover, would probably bring deficits in the current account quickly back to the fore and thus restrain future growth. Even in a Greece that has been devastated by the crisis and the policies imposed on it by the EU, there are signs that current account deficits are returning in 2014, i.e., as soon as the economy's contraction had ceased.

Pursuing the issue further, Figure 4 shows that among the core countries and the biggest traders of the EMU the relationship between ULC and the current account during the critical period from 1999 to 2007 is both clearly visible and negative.

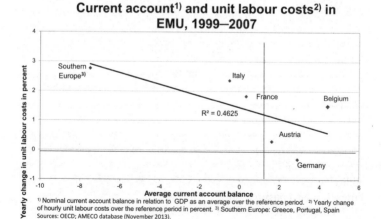

Current account[1] and unit labour costs[2] in EMU, 1999–2007

[1] Nominal current account balance in relation to GDP as an average over the reference period. [2] Yearly change of hourly unit labour costs over the reference period in percent. [3] Southern Europe: Greece, Portugal, Spain
Sources: OECD; AMECO database (November 2013).

Fig. 4: Trade imbalances, prices and wages

The relationship would be even stronger if, instead of ULC, the movement of prices (i.e., the GDP deflator) was compared to the movement of the current account, as is shown in Figure 5.

Current account[1] and inflation[2] in EMU, 1999—2007

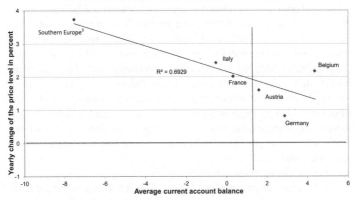

[1] Nominal current account balance in relation to GDP as an average over the reference period. [2] Yearly change of GDP deflator over the reference period in percent. [3] Southern Europe: Greece, Portugal, Spain
Sources: OECD; AMECO database (November 2013)

Fig. 5: Trade imbalances, prices and wages

Note: Negative values represent a current account deficit
Source: AMECO database (as per Nov-12); own calculations

The countries included in both of these figures account for close to 80 percent of overall EMU trade (internal and external). Furthermore, for Italy and France, the most important competitor inside and outside EMU is Germany. To assume that an accumulated price difference of 20 percent to 30 percent, such as has taken place since the start of the EMU, would not influence trade to the benefit of Germany is complete nonsense. The conclusion drawn is absolutely unjustified: 'The developments in unit labour costs are endogenous and partly determined by capital flows. This may suggest that the Euro Plus Pact may have limited ability to impact unit labour costs and even if possible, this may have little effect on a possible emergence of current account imbalances.'[5]

Finally, the need to avoid imbalances within a currency union is not mainly about current account deficits and surpluses per se in a clearly

5   See Gabrisch, et al., 2014.

defined period of time. The point is, rather, that absolute and cumulative advantages of one country or a group of countries against a similar country or group of countries are definitively unsustainable over very long time spans. A huge gap in competitiveness and the resulting losses in market shares would have to be closed at some point, because otherwise the losing country or region would find it impossible to persuade its lenders that it would be able to repay its debts at some point in the future. Whether this point will be reached in twenty years or in forty years is not important for a nation depending on the capital market. The fact that it will happen is sufficient to trigger the reactions of the market that we have seen in all financial crises.

The calculus of the market is simple: Final repayment of any international debt is payment in kind. If it is not permanently to impoverish the debtor countries, such repayment requires a gain in market share, that is, the emergence of a current account surplus in the debtor country and of a deficit on the creditor's side. An indebted country could only service and repay its debt over time if the surplus country allowed the deficit country to begin to register surpluses at some point. The change could only occur by means of changes in competitiveness that would occur through price adjustments resulting from wage adjustments and/or changes in the exchange rate. Quantity adjustments in international trade cannot be a permanent solution.

Unlike capitalist enterprises, countries typically neither go bankrupt, nor disappear. They are obliged to find ways of coping with situations where nearly all their productive agents face absolute disadvantages against their competitors abroad. The most direct and brutal way to deal with high unit labour costs (in international currency) would be to reduce wages. If it were possible to reduce nominal wages only in those parts of the economy that were exposed to international competition, many negative side effects could be avoided for the rest of the economy. Currency depreciation would do exactly that. A declining currency would reduce nominal wages expressed in international currency, but not across the board in all sectors of the economy. Imports would become more expensive and they would tend to be replaced by domestically produced products; exports would become cheaper for international clients and would tend to increase. Even if imports (of commodities) could not be replaced at all by domestic products, however, the international adjustment of wages would be unavoidable to allow the country to buy the necessary imports through its own exports.

⊠. Competition among Nations?

One of the most intriguing issues of the last several decades has been that of competition among nations – or 'the battle of nations' – in the field of trade. The age of globalisation, more than any other before, has been interpreted as a period in which nations are compelled to compete in similar ways to capitalist enterprises. The wealth of nations is often considered to depend on a nation's ability effectively to adjust to the challenges thrown out by the open markets for commodities and for capital. Nations with a high capital endowment are typically expected to come under competitive pressure from trading partners with low wages and weak labour standards. In particular, the existence of a huge pool of idle labour in large developing economies, such as China and India, is assumed fundamentally to alter the capital/labour ratio for the world as a whole in favour of capital, thus leading to a new global wage equilibrium.

Reality appears to have confirmed this expectation. Wages in many high-wage countries of the North have come under pressure, and labour has failed to appropriate the share of productivity growth that it had managed for several decades before – capital has won. Wage shares in GDP have been falling, and trust in the ability of market economies to ensure full participation of all people in the progress of society at large has been fading. However, the fact that wage shares have been on the decline does not mean that the forces driving this phenomenon are those typically included in the neoliberal model of the labour market, which is the ultimate source of the idea that the cause of lower wages in many industrialised economies is pressure from emerging markets.

A closer look reveals the limits and weaknesses of that idea, for it it assumes that competition among entire economies functions in the same way as competition among enterprises. This analogy is out of place. The model capturing competition among enterprises does not apply to countries, especially not to countries with independent currencies. In the dynamic setting of a market economy, enterprises compete by improving the productivity of their labour. Supply side conditions – in particular the prices for intermediate goods, labour and capital – are normally alike and given for enterprises within a country. Consequently, an individual enterprise's success or failure is determined by the value that is specifically added at the enterprise level to the inputs mobilised.

Enterprises as price takers generally have to accept the going prices for labour with variable qualifications, in the same way that they have to accept the price of capital. Enterprises that are able to raise productivity through innovation and by introducing new products would normally operate with lower unit labour costs than their competitors. Consequently, they would be able to offer their goods at lower prices, or to make higher profits at given prices. The former implies gaining market share, the latter may mean gaining strategic long-term advantages through higher investment ratios. If the prices of labour and intermediary products are given, competitors would have to adjust by implementing the same, or a similar, technology; the alternative would be to leave the market because their activities would be no longer viable economically.

This fundamental mechanism of competition does not apply at the level of countries because wage rates are normally set at the national level. Unlike enterprises, countries are wage setters rather than wage takers, whether that is due to mobility of labour within a country, or due to wage negotiations at a national level. If wages are negotiated at the national level, or if labour is geographically mobile, the so-called law of one price, i.e., equal pay for equal work, would have to be applied, which means that all enterprises, irrespective of their profitability or efficiency, would have to pay the same wage. Consequently, stronger growth of productivity at the level of a national economy would not increase the competitiveness of all its enterprises relative to the rest of the world. Economy-wide productivity progress would normally be reflected in higher nominal wages (and real wages) and unchanged unit labour cost growth.

But, even if this mechanism did not work – for whatever reason – a country with generally high productivity but extremely low wages and very low unit labour costs would not automatically increase its international competitiveness, nor the competitiveness of all its enterprises. Expressed in international currency, the prices of a country that consistently used wage-dumping policies to raise its international competitiveness would not necessarily be lower than in the rest of the world. In a world of national currencies and national monetary policy, a country supplying its goods at much lower prices would gain market share as well as accumulating huge trade and current account surpluses. However, at the same time, political pressure to adjust wages and prices in terms of international currency would mount. Sooner or later, that country would be forced to adjust its wages measured in international currency by allowing an appreciation of its currency.

Nations could open their borders to both trade and capital flows, if they could be assured that their enterprises would have fair opportunities in the global division of labour and that they would not be in danger of permanently losing out against the rest of the world. This simple proposition underlies all international trade arrangements, made in the WTO and elsewhere. If, at the level of the national economy, the nominal remuneration of labour – which is typically labour as the immobile factor of production – exceeded the effectiveness of its use (i.e., labour productivity) consistently and by a wider margin than in competing countries, the country in question would face major difficulties because most of its enterprises would be in trouble. They would either have to ask for higher prices and thus accept the permanent loss of market share, or they would have to accept lower profits to avoid the loss of market share. Such a state of affairs, which would be the result of the appreciation and overvaluation of the real exchange rate, would be unsustainable. As a rule of thumb, once the accumulated overvaluation rose to 20 percent or so, a crisis would become unavoidable. The most visible indicator of this pathological situation, though not its cause, would be a deficit in the current account balance. The real problems would arise if the government decided to put downward pressure on wages, making it impossible to revive the economy and leading the country to deflationary conditions. If several countries adopted this approach, generalised deflation would become unavoidable. This logic is beginning to dominate in the Eurozone as inflation rates have fallen clearly and consistently below the ECB target for a prolonged period of time in 2013 and 2014.

Italy and the United Kingdom faced problems of similar nature as members of the EMS in 1992. Italy opted to remain within the system and the United Kingdom opted to leave it, but both devalued their currency. In systems of adjustable exchange rates the way out of a balance of payments crisis is rather simple: the currency of the country in trouble has to devalue, thereby restoring a competitive level of nominal wages and nominal unit labour costs measured in international currency. In countries participating in monetary unions and thus unable to devalue, however, recovering competitiveness is an entirely different story.

▨. Germany's Success – and Its failure

It is conceivable that some readers might be irritated at this stage of the proceedings. For, is it not reasonable to say that Germany is the only country inside EMU that has got everything right? It is politically strong, its economic performance is impressive and, as the main creditor country, it dictates the terms at which the debtor countries may receive financial assistance. From the point of view of this book, however, the judgement about wrongdoers and violators of the Maastricht Treaty is quite different. We have shown already that German wage restraint violated the commonly agreed inflation target. The conclusion that Germany has been delinquent is inevitable once it is acknowledged that unit labour costs, rather than monetary aggregates, are the main determinant of inflation within a country as well as for the monetary union as a whole.

Furthermore, when making a judgement about whether the German approach was really successful, it is also necessary to consider the reasons why Germany was able to take advantage of a historically unique situation, including the naïveté of its partner countries during the first ten years of EMU. Why was it possible for wage restraint – making real wages lag far behind productivity – to become such a powerful instrument for Germany? Is this the final proof of the validity of neoliberal labour market theory?

To answer these questions, it is necessary to differentiate between, on the one hand, the effects of wage restraint on export performance and, on the other, its effects on the domestic economy. This distinction is necessary because there can be no doubt that a large country with intense trade relations with its neighbours could gain extraordinarily if it 'beggared' these neighbours for a long time by essentially robbing them of significant market share in regional and in global trade. Indeed, Germany's share of exports in GDP, which had been rather stable at 30 percent of GDP for several decades before the creation of EMU, exploded during the rather short time span from 1999 to 2013 to peak at more than 50 percent.

It is an integral part of Keynesian theory that 'beggaring' one's neighbours could be a successful strategy as long as the trading partners accepted this form of economic imperialism and did not undertake retaliatory action.[6] The EMU, as an implicit part of the free trade

---

6   See especially the famous Chapter 19 of Keynes, 1936.

arrangements of the EU, failed to confront this problem in an effective manner for two reasons. First, because its macroeconomic implications were ignored due to the doctrinal and theoretical obsessions discussed earlier; second, because the other countries of the monetary union were unable to retaliate against the aggressive German approach either through trade policies, or through depreciation. The strict common market free trade agreements of the EU and the very existence of the EMU prevented their response. It was only under these unique circumstances that the German strategy could prove immensely successful on the external front for several years.

On the domestic side, however, the German approach was a complete failure. The wage restraint strategy originally aimed at stimulating the creation of a large number of jobs by changing relative factor prices as well as by restructuring of production in the direction of more labour intensive processes. This strategy, drawing on the neoliberal understanding of the labour market, never succeeded. Its failure was caused, first, because the underlying theoretical approach ignores the time dimension and, second, because a wage cut, or a slowdown of wage growth, would be followed in reality by a fall in domestic demand.[7]

The neoliberal wage–employment nexus, according to which a wage reduction would induce a change in the structure of production, assumes that overall demand would not change after the wage reduction. That is, neoliberal theory assumes what must never be assumed in a capitalist economy, i.e., the independence of supply and demand in the labour market. In a closed economy, or in an economy with a small external sector, a drop in the aggregate sum of wages and, thus, a reduction of the aggregate demand of workers' households could only be avoided if employment increased at exactly the same rate as wages fell. Moreover, this balancing out would have to be accomplished instantaneously, in a 'theoretical second'. If there were any frictions in the restructuring of production, or any lags in the adjustment of employment, the wage–employment nexus suggested by neoliberal theory would collapse.

The flaws of the neoliberal nexus would become obvious if real time and the sequence of events were considered. Cutting wages would immediately reduce the aggregate demand by workers' households; with the synchronised fall in wages and in demand by wage earners, enterprises

---

7   For further analysis of this point see UNCTAD, Trade and Development Report 2012, and Flassbeck, 2013.

would become unwilling to invest; new investment, however, would be absolutely required to restructure production in light of the new relative prices of labour and capital; with falling demand and declining capacity utilisation of the existing capital stock, investment in fixed capital would also fall thus weakening domestic demand further. The end result would be that unemployment would rise rather than fall. This is precisely what happened in Greece, Portugal and Spain after wages were forced to fall by the conditions set by the troika, as is shown in Figure 6.

In the four countries, put together, pressure on nominal wages (right-hand scale) started in 2008 with the growth rate flattening visibly. The real wage per hour started to fall in absolute terms in 2010 from an average level of 17 euros. With the absolute reduction in real wages to close to 16 euros per hour, unemployment continued to rise nearly at the same pace as before (during the global crisis). That can only be explained by the immediate negative effect falling wages have on domestic demand. Instead of pricing themselves back into the market, workers accepting falling wages price themselves out of the market because they cannot any longer buy the products that they are producing.

A similar process also happened in Germany as domestic demand remained flat for many years reflecting the stagnation in real wages. It

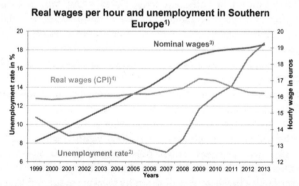

Real wages per hour and unemployment in Southern Europe[1]

1) Greece, Italy, Portugal, Spain. 2) Left-hand scale: Unemployed in percent of total labour force, Eurostat definition. 3) Right-hand scale: Gross income of emplyees per hour worked. 4) Right-hand scale: Nominal wage per hour, price adjusted by private consumption deflator.
Sources: OECD; AMECO database; 2013 values based on EU Commission forecast; working hours for Italy: own estimations.

Fig. 6: Unemployment and real wages

was only due to the extraordinary success in international trade that Germany could be considered successful overall. In effect, observers are impressed by the German experiment because the country benefitted tremendously from its 'beggar-thy-neighbour' strategy during the years immediately preceding the financial crisis.

Indeed, absolute advantages in competitiveness, such as those achieved by Germany, accumulate over time. The bigger the absolute advantage, the greater the gain in market shares in a fast-growing global economy. The stupendous increase in Germany's export share in GDP and its export surplus reflect an unprecedented and unrepeatable explosion of exports. For many German observers, Germany's gain in political strength following the crisis is even more impressive than its economic performance per se. However, much of this strength is due to the simple fact that during a financial crisis (when agents become extremely risk averse) debtor countries, which typically depend on foreign capital, usually are on the defensive, while creditor countries gain the upper hand.

Germany's extraordinary success in international trade was in large part due to the numbness of Germany's neighbours and to the blindness of the institutions created to guide and oversee the Eurozone's functioning, particularly the ECB and the European Commission. A more vigilant central bank or a more attentive EU Commission would have probably intervened earlier in the day, warning Germany of the risks of its strategy and alerting its neighbours. Their failure is a direct result of the ideological pillars on which EMU has been built: in the early 1980s, the Commission adopted neoliberalism with religious assiduity, allowing it to guide its decisions and actions since then. After all, improving competitiveness has been the declared target of the EU as a whole. Under these circumstances, how could the Commission hinder Germany from doing what everybody else was expected to do?

The institutional failure is even more severe in the case of the ECB. If it had had its eyes open and if there had been no ideological barriers, the ECB would have recognised from its early days that nominal unit labour cost, not the money supply, is the main determinant of inflation for the union as a whole as well as for the member states. The ECB failed to analyse the overall macroeconomic developments and to spot the emergence of major disequilibria. It also failed to anticipate the possible deflationary outcomes in case of a crisis. The ECB, as an independent institution, could have mitigated the disaster that has ensued since 2010 by using its political influence, or by issuing public warnings that the EMU was on a dangerous path.

In the course of the year 2014, the general reception of the crisis by the ECB has changed quite remarkably. Time and again, has its president mentioned the need for more expansionary fiscal policies in the surplus countries and even hinted to higher wages in those countries that could afford it to support the ECB in its fight against deflation. To change the political course, however, Mario Draghi has to speak up and name the wrongdoers explicitly. A coalition of opposing countries with substantive support from the most important institution would definitively impress German politics and would open the way for an honest and serious discussion inside the country.

⊠. GERMANY HAS TO ADJUST

It is plausible to argue (even by someone sympathetic to the views expressed in this book) that, for Germany, the strategy to contain domestic nominal wage growth was not motivated primarily by competition inside EMU but rather with emerging economies, in particular the rising industrial power of China. It might even be added that this strategy was fully in line with the general orientation of the European Union for several years, urging its members to improve their competitiveness.

Although these arguments would be intuitively attractive, they would be fallacious because they would overlook, once again, the crucial importance of the strong and stable relationship between the growth rate of unit labour costs and the inflation rate, on the one hand, and the growth rate of real wages and domestic demand, on the other. Under no circumstances should a monetary union trying to achieve an inflation rate of 2 percent allow one of its member countries (particularly the biggest one) to go its own way in terms of ULC development and inflation. If Europe felt that there was a challenge from emerging markets, which had to be addressed at the macroeconomic level, it could have chosen a lower inflation rate (or even deflation) as the target of its common monetary policy. However, in that case, the exchange rate of the Euro against the Chinese Yuan, or the US Dollar, would have reflected sooner or later the lower inflation in Europe, thus destroying the advantage that Europe would have tried to obtain by pursuing a lower inflation target.

In a world of floating or adjustable exchange rates, no country could gain a permanent advantage against another country, if the latter had the option of adjusting its exchange rate in accordance with inflation differentials. This means that all attempts to improve competitiveness by cutting or moderating wages for the EMU as a whole would be useless. And yet, this is precisely the approach that Europe has chosen as a way forward after the crisis. This is deeply misguided also because in most European debtor countries wage cuts would lead to severe falls in domestic demand, which is more important than external demand. In economies with an export share in GDP that was far below 50 percent, wage restraint strategies would be counterproductive, since there would not be a realistic prospect of achieving a huge current account surplus over a lengthy period of time, and nor would it be possible to raise the export share in GDP beyond the 50 percent mark without suffering retaliation from trading partners. Under normal circumstances, it would therefore be impossible to successfully emulate the strategy followed by Germany during the first ten years of EMU.

Even more important than these general objections regarding German strategy, however, would be the dynamics of the overall economy. In a monetary union, a country with a low export share and facing a huge current account deficit and financing problems due to an implicitly overvalued currency would be trapped. Downward adjustment of wages, sometimes erroneously called 'internal devaluation', would be no solution as it would destroy both domestic demand and output before it could bring some relief through rising exports.

Furthermore, countries with a huge gap of competitiveness against Germany would have to go through an extended period of catching-up in terms of price competitiveness. There would be neither rapid gains in international market share, nor a lasting improvement in the current account position, since Germany's absolute advantage would remain intact as long as the competitiveness gap was not turned into the opposite, i.e., an absolute advantage of the deficit countries. Figure 1 has already shown that deficit countries have to dive below the German UCL path for a long time to regain some of the losses they have experienced in the first ten years of EMU.

The Achilles heel of this adjustment process is its duration. A democratic country could not possibly sustain five to ten years of falling living standards and rising unemployment. The economic, social and political costs would be tremendous, as is made clear for Greece in this book. The process would result in social upheaval, including desperate attempts by the people to use elections to prevent what would be in their eyes a frivolous attack on their well-being.

This is why the adjustment process within the EMU would have to be symmetrical at the very least. This means that the country that has implicitly undervalued its exchange rate – Germany – would have to engage in a strong effort of upward adjustment, i.e., faster wage increases, while other countries would undertake a slowly downward adjustment. The most reliable yardstick for the success of the adjustment efforts on both sides would be the inflation target again. If the common inflation target was not questioned, to restore the deficit countries' international competitiveness it would be necessary to raise ULC and inflation in the surplus country up to the point where external balance on both sides over the entire life of the monetary union (the first ten years included) would be achieved. It is enough merely to state this requirement to make its extraordinary difficulty absolutely apparent.

CHAPTER 4

The Stock-Flow Quandary of the EMU

⊠. Politics Tends to Focus on Stocks but Flows are Even More Crucial

Since the outbreak of the crisis, a lot of political energy has been devoted in the Eurozone to dealing with the problem of stocks, whether these are bad loans, an apparently unsustainable government debt, or the balance sheet of shaky banks. Much less political enthusiasm has been invested in turning around flows, and more specifically income (growth), investment and consumption. To tackle a crisis by mainly addressing stocks is exactly the wrong way to proceed, for future stocks are the result of today's flows. To avoid the creation of new problematic stocks, priority has to be given to restoring flows, even if this inflicts some pain on the holders of today's stocks.

In an economy characterised by unsustainable foreign debt that has been accumulated over many years due to a loss in competitiveness and falling market share, debt seems to be the most urgent problem at first glance. If, for example, the financing of imports through the capital market was at risk, or became extremely costly, and international reserves approached depletion, a country would need emergency assistance because flows of exports and imports could not be adjusted overnight. However, it ought not be stressed that even the immediate financing of imports would be a part of a strategy of restoring flows rather than dealing with stocks.

In past currency crises, such as those in Latin America and Asia in the 1980s and 1990s, the IMF had to step in because the countries in crisis were unable to stop the outflow of funds and the collapse of their currencies. When the IMF stepped in – albeit with unnecessary and even useless 'conditionality' – the main effect was to support the short-term financing of imports. As the devaluation of the national currency improved a country's competitiveness over time, the turnaround of the country's economy would occur through increased exports and reduced imports. The rebalancing typically became feasible as higher prices for imports induced the substitution of many imports by domestic goods, so that the need to finance imports was reduced. As the current account turned to surplus, the financing needs disappeared and so did the need to rely on IMF assistance.

The EMU crisis, if one abstracts from the existence of the common currency and the institutions that support it, is very similar to a foreign exchange crisis. A moment's reflection would show that the provision of finance to countries with current account deficits ought to be much easier, whereas the switch from imports to domestic products and the stimulation of exports would be much more difficult. In a properly functioning monetary union a country should not face difficulties in financing its imports and, furthermore, such difficulties would not in any case occur in the same form as in a system of floating currencies. In a currency union, the financial markets would sanction current account deficits that appear to have become unsustainable mainly by requiring much higher interest rates on government bonds. This would be the case even in situations in which government debt would not itself be the main problem, simply because the government would be the only entity that the markets could clearly identify as being 'national'. The government would therefore be taken as the culprit of the trouble that the respective economy would face as a whole.

Governments do not, of course, go bankrupt in the same way as enterprises. However, in a world of national currencies, the traditional sanction of the markets in the course of a crisis would be to 'ask' for higher interest rates to compensate for the increasing risk of currency devaluation, the latter being the main risk facing foreigners holding the government debt. Once the crisis of the Eurozone hit, it was typically observed that interest rates on government debt of peripheral and other countries rose rapidly, even though there was no risk of currency devaluation. In countries with a low stock of government debt, like in Ireland and in Spain, the same logic applied as in Greece with its high stock of government debt. There was no risk of default in the case of Spain and a risk of default was only later introduced into the system by the decision of the troika to allow the partial default of the Greek government debt. Thus, observers of the crisis often confused the dire straits of a country for those of its government. The consequent policy response was immediately to tackle the problem of the stock of public debt, and for long to ignore the country's flow problems. This was absolutely the wrong approach.

Even under floating exchange rates, there is often a harsh conflict between stock and flow adjustments. It is impossible to overestimate the severity of the difficulties that would be faced by individuals and institutions in a country that was under threat of devaluation who held open positions or were indebted in a foreign currency. In the run-up to the Argentine crisis in 2001, for example, many individuals as well as the government were indebted in US dollars. Thus, they feared the threat of a sharp devaluation of the peso (which had been fixed to the dollar at a rate of 1:1 for nearly ten years by that time) which would lead to an explosion of private and government debt, if that were expressed in national currency. Consequently, the Argentine government attempted to defend the parity of the peso with the dollar by all means and for a long time. However, a country in deep recession and with an overvalued currency needs a demand stimulus, and such a stimulus could be provided by currency devaluation, whatever happens to stocks. In the end, the complete breakdown of Argentina's 'currency board' system (with a fixed exchange rate vis-à-vis the dollar) could not be avoided.

In the EMU, things are more complicated, but the underlying logic is similar. When a country is forced into 'internal devaluation', i.e., wage cuts, to improve its international competitiveness, the deflationary effect of this policy would increase the real value of both domestic and foreign debt because the nominal value of the debt would remain unchanged while income flows would be reduced. If a country was forced to leave the monetary union and to devalue its new currency, the same logic would apply as in the case of floating exchange rates. At the same time, surplus countries would enjoy the benefit of lower interest rates on government debt. Furthermore, in these countries the real value of all debts, including those of the government, would fall, if adjustment took the form of 'internal revaluation', i.e., of higher wages, higher unit labour costs, and higher inflation over time.

The need to deal with flows as a matter of priority becomes even more apparent from a different perspective. If dealing with unsustainable debt was attempted merely through adjusting stocks and without strengthening flows, it would simply lead to failure. In Greece, for example, there was a 'haircut' of government debt in 2011–12, which completely failed to improve the overall economic situation and to reduce government debt over time, because the economy actually took a turn for the worse due to austerity and wage cuts.

Moreover, if a country reduced its government debt significantly by declaring a default, it would be essential to realise that the holders of the government debt would suffer wealth losses exactly mirroring the gains of the government. If the losers were domestic holders of debt, as was overwhelmingly the case in Greece in 2011–12, domestic demand would be likely to suffer. Private expenditure would be reduced and the contractionary effect could be countered only if the propensity to consume somehow rose, or investment increased significantly. But even if the holders of the government debt were mainly located in other countries, it would be hard to imagine that a government that adopted such a harsh measure would be able to stimulate its own economy immediately and significantly (for instance, by increasing its deficits) without facing renewed sanctions from financial markets. In short, dealing with unsustainable debt by focusing primarily, or even exclusively, on the stock of debt is a harsh and problematic option.

Note that most of the effects discussed above are symmetrical between the deficit and the surplus country, or between the depreciating and the appreciating country. A currency appreciation would normally take place within a very short time period, and it would typically be the result of a forced and chaotic adjustment. The appreciating country would face a higher valuation of its stocks, but its flows would necessarily suffer as exports would become more expensive in international currency and imports would become cheaper in national currency. Thus, there would be considerable pain of adjustment for the surplus country too.

The point is that, in a monetary union, the removal of a competitiveness gap through larger wage increases in the surplus countries and smaller wage increases (or even no wage increases at all) in the deficit countries could be stretched over a long period of time, and would thus be much less harmful to economies. The pivotal country for such a policy would be Germany. If Germany were willing to adopt a plan of coordinated wage adjustment policies, the structural change involved would not necessarily overstretch the ability of individuals and enterprises to adjust. To be specific, wage growth in Germany should be accelerated to the point where real wages would move in tandem with productivity, while inflation would be in line with the ECB target. The growth of real wages would improve the purchasing power of consumers in Germany, including for imports. If nominal wage increases were even stronger (i.e., higher than productivity growth plus the common inflation target) the time needed for overall European adjustment would be even shorter.

A policy of this nature would deal with flows, achieving a slow but steady solution of the competitiveness gap problem, and providing a boost to other economies through rising German demand. Even such a solution, however, would need a considerable length of time to heal the imbalances that have emerged during the first ten years of the EMU. It would not be unreasonable to expect that it would take ten to twenty years to reach a situation in which all countries would be able to achieve growth of income that would be based on their underlying economic strength and would be unimpeded by constraints to finance imports. Unfortunately the social and political alliances for such a turn of policy in Germany and the rest of Europe do not exist at present.

The crucial point lies with the very nature of a currency union. The unification of money in a system of fiat money ultimately rests on the trust invested in the institutions that manage paper money and are obliged to guarantee its value. Trust cannot be split into regional entities, and nor could there be different levels of trust within a monetary union. Trust is either everywhere or nowhere. In a properly functioning monetary union, trust in the authorities could be grounded merely on their promise to stabilise the value of money. It would also depend on their ability to prevent disequilibria among member countries resulting from divergences in competitiveness. It would further depend on the willingness of the authorities to ensure stable growth and high employment, allowing each member economy to 'stand on its own feet'. The EMU has failed all these crucial tests, instead becoming a vehicle for German economic and political domination of Europe due to the application of a flawed theoretical approach.

⬛. With Forced Adjustment of Competitiveness, Deflation Becomes the Main threat

The process of adjustment now underway in the EMU – as proposed and enforced by the 'troika', (i.e., the ECB, the European Commission and the IMF) – has gone in exactly the opposite direction to that discussed above. The troika has started from the assumption that Germany, the main creditor country, has pursued the right policies, while the debtor countries have done everything wrong. However, as was shown above, blaming the debtors and favouring the creditors is clearly unjustified in the case of EMU. Asymmetric adjustment – i.e., wage cuts and deflation in deficit countries but unchanged policies in Germany – is a recipe for disaster. Competitiveness is a relative concept and if all countries try to improve competitiveness by cutting wages, the result would be a race to the bottom. In that race, no country could improve its condition, but rather everyone would lose because domestic demand in the union as a whole would fall.

The proper criterion for judging policies in the member countries of the EMU must be the common inflation target. If EMU authorities are determined to stick to the agreed inflation target of 2 percent for the union as a whole, Germany must deviate upwards from the target, allowing for wage increases that would exceed its productivity path and resulting in a rise in unit labour costs temporarily above the common inflation target. At the same time, other countries have to lower the rate of ULC growth they have experienced in the past.

At present the EMU is at risk of falling into a deflationary trap. If Germany failed to deliver wage increases that were clearly above 4 percent (note that wage agreements concluded in 2014 were far below this mark, and 2015 is unlikely to bring a major change) wages in other countries, especially France and Italy, would have to fall in absolute terms. This would badly hurt their economies, increasing unemployment due to the fall in domestic demand, and thus exacerbating political turmoil. Given that southern European countries, including Spain, have gone to quite some lengths in cutting wages, and given that Germany is refusing to move in the opposite direction, conditions have become dramatically worse for France and Italy. If they attempt to stick to the commonly agreed inflation target in the future, they would be severely squeezed between the still very competitive Germany and the southern European countries whose competitiveness has improved.

Hence, the most probable outcome is deflation across the Eurozone, with France and Italy being forced to follow southern Europe sooner or later – at least if the EMU continues to exist. Deflation has become clearly visible in the EMU since the second half of 2013, with price increases falling below the 2 percent line and even below 1 percent. It is worth stressing that the ECB, even if it used its tools more aggressively, would have limited power to combat a wage-driven deflation.

Given the current configuration of European politics, the crucial political question becomes: How long could democracy continue to function if one government after another became unable to stimulate the economy and to reduce unemployment? If history can be any guide, it teaches us a simple lesson: After many fruitless attempts to stick to the rules and play the game dictated by the creditors, a point would be reached when the government of a debtor country would face the prospect of political and social collapse. At that point, a country would finally have to do what has to be done for survival.

One option would be to form a coalition within the EMU that would put pressure on Germany to adjust symmetrically. But such pressure would only be credible if the coalition were able to threaten Germany with a realistic option. That could only be to leave the monetary union, introduce a national currency and allow for a sharp devaluation. Such a step would be unprecedented and is likely to be associated with tremendous short-term frictions. However, given the current outlook of Europe, it is likely that a time will come when it becomes unavoidable. That is why preparing technically, socially and politically for such an eventuality is indispensable for responsible politics in Europe at the moment. The modalities and implications of this option – particularly for peripheral countries and focusing on Greece – are discussed at some length in the rest of this book.

▨. THE ROLE OF FISCAL DEFICITS AND NATIONAL FINANCIAL FLOWS IN GERMANY

Since the start of EMU, fiscal retrenchment – i.e., efforts to reduce public deficits and public debt, under the label of 'sound macroeconomic policies' – has been the mantra of European policy makers and economic analysts. This policy stance has been considered crucial to freeing the spirit of markets and of entrepreneurship. In reality, it never had this significance. Markets and states can perfectly well coexist, and indeed they could complement each other for their mutual benefit. Moreover, fiscal targets would be of secondary or even tertiary importance for a monetary union.

As was elaborated above, inflation is mainly determined by the growth in nominal unit labour costs, and by monetary policy dealing with the technical aspects of money markets and intermediary financial institutions. In normal times, the role of public spending would be mainly to allocate sufficient resources for provision of public goods, to ensure fair and efficient taxation, and to employ productively that part of disposable capital that would not be absorbed by the private sector. Public finance would have no direct impact either on inflation or on the external balance.

But times are rarely normal. With an unsettled economic outlook, high and rising unemployment, and economic policy doctrines that focus on minimising the role of government and of the state in general, public budgets have increasingly become the hinge between the state and the market. They have an impact, for better or worse, on the integration of national economies into the world economy.

In a seminal book, Richard Koo has shown that financial crises would tend to end up in 'balance sheet recessions'.[1] If such a recession materialised, it would become absolutely imperative for the government to intervene, and the reason is plain. If enterprises and private households were keen to repair their balance sheets following a financial crisis, they would eagerly cut expenditure and would not respond to monetary stimuli in the normal way by increasing credit-financed expenditure. Private households are typically net savers, and thus a country would be able to escape a balance sheet recession without sharply increasing its fiscal deficits only if it could rely on other countries to be its debtors. That is precisely the situation of Germany relative to the rest of the EMU.

If this was impossible (as would be the case for most countries) the government would have to step in and deal with savings that were not automatically transformed into investment, but existed as hoards tending to depress the whole economy, and thereby to increase government deficits. In short, the government must proactively replace the missing borrowers and investors in the private sector. The same would hold for economies facing pressures from high unemployment, an unequal income distribution, stagnating wages, and very high and rising profits, as was shown in previous chapters.

The interplay of saving and investment could also be analysed to a certain extent by examining the net financial flows among the different sectors of the economy. These flows, if the rest of the world is included, add up to zero since the world as a whole cannot have deficits or surpluses. Germany, more than any other country in the EMU, is the crucial case to consider in this context, as it appears to have solved the problem of stimulating demand without sacrificing its fiscal thriftiness.

---

1   See Koo, 2008.

Figure 7 depicts the pattern of net financial flows in Germany over the past fifty years. In the 1960s (shown in the figure on the left) the net borrowing of the corporate sector was the main counterpart to the net savings of households. During that period, neither the government nor foreign countries significantly contributed to the absorption of private savings. However, in the 2000s and following the introduction of the EMU (shown in the figure on the right) a totally different world emerged. The German corporate sector increasingly moved away from its traditional deficit position to assume a role as net saver. At the beginning of the first decade of EMU the government was still in deficit. However, in 2009, it decided virtually to cease its current net borrowing by introducing a 'debt break' into the German constitution that would henceforth allow only for very small amounts of annual net borrowing by the state.

The inevitable counterpart of the attempt by all sectors of the German economy to become net savers has been growing indebtedness of foreign countries to German lenders. The mechanism that has allowed Germany to achieve this extraordinary outcome has been examined in detail in earlier chapters, including the real depreciation via wage dumping initiated by government and employer pressure on

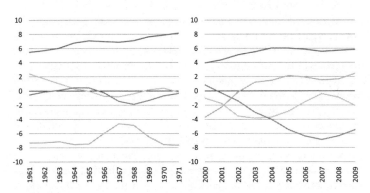

Fig. 7: Net financial flows[1] in Germany[2]

Note:
1 Net debt position of a business sector in relation to gross national product; moving three-year averages
2 Western Germany until 1991; Germany starting 1991
Sources: German Federal Ministry of Finance; AMECO database (as per May 2011); own calculations

the trade unions. The result for the EMU has been disastrous, while the result for the German economy has been to adopt an unsustainable growth trajectory that poses an enormous problem for economic policy.

The challenge for Germany is to coax its enterprises back into conditions in which they earn much less but invest much more. The incredible increase in German profits during the second half of the first decade of EMU has been due to the tremendous success of German enterprises in Europe and across the world, mostly at the expense of their European neighbours. It has been shown in this book that, in the absence of the export channel, the German experiment of wage restraint would have been a complete failure since it substantially slowed domestic demand. Nor would the accumulation of profits have been possible without export growth that was largely driven by Germany's real depreciation. With the export channel wide open, German enterprises that specialise in tradable goods used the golden opportunity to expand their market share and their profit share at the same time. The EMU has been tremendously beneficial to German exporting capital, but not to German workers and households.

Since most of the former importers of German goods in Europe are in dire straits and no longer willing to assume the role of debtor, the policy followed by Germany has to be changed radically. Policy makers have options that are based on wages and taxes. A restructuring of aggregate demand towards strengthening domestic and weakening foreign demand has to be achieved. Reversing wage restraint and securing an extended period of wage growth is the first and most important measure. However, it is natural to expect ferocious opposition from employers, particularly from exporting enterprises. Strong government intervention would be crucial to achieving the required shift in the balance of power in the labour market in favour of labour. At the same time, the government would have to restore corporate tax rates at normal levels, using the proceeds for infrastructure investments and thereby benefitting enterprises that specialise in domestic investment and in satisfying domestic demand.

The task ahead for Germany is all the more challenging as the entirety of its economic policy is based on achieving export surpluses. 'Export orientation' is defended tooth and claw in German politics and in the media, described as the only way for the economy to prosper and create jobs. But German policy makers (and enterprises) have to learn the lesson that other nations cannot be used systematically as debtors, only to be subsequently dismissed as 'lax', 'lazy' and 'flippant' in their economic behaviour. Germany has to question the foundations of its own economic model. This mental shift is particularly difficult to achieve when the need for a new economic policy orientation has not been triggered by an external event, such as a currency appreciation. In the context of the currency union, the German shift must be initiated internally by acknowledging that the model chosen in the 1990s has turned out to be unsustainable. However, given the political and social implications, it would be unreasonable to expect such a process to occur in Germany in the foreseeable future.

The only force that could shake Germany from its complacency would be combined political pressure by other European countries, including France. Alternatively, Germany could wake up if the walls began to crumble in one country of the EMU after another, possibly leading to a looming panic in several countries at the same time. If they recognised not their individual weakness but their collective power, a coalition of debtor countries led by France and threatening to bring the end of EMU may be the only way to force Germany to change its economic model without a social and economic catastrophe across Europe. For, if the EMU came to an end, the new currencies of debtor countries – and France – would be devalued significantly relative to the old Euro and to the new German currency, thus destroying a huge part of German export markets overnight.

CHAPTER 5

European and Global Inability to Deal with External Imbalances

◻. THE EU'S MACROECONOMIC IMBALANCE PROCEDURE AND ITS BIASED EXECUTION

The European Commission took the decision to launch an in-depth review of the German current account surplus and to include Germany into the proceedings of the Europe 'Six Pack', which includes the Macroeconomic Imbalance Procedure, initiated in 2011. These steps were positive steps but it should be kept in mind that the action of the Commission was taken under enormous political pressure from Germany. Thus, the decision to treat surpluses differently from deficits on current account (surpluses to be reviewed at 6 percent of GDP, while deficits at 4 percent) was not justified at all.

Meanwhile, the first In-Depth Reports (IDR) have already been published and the results make for sober reading. Looking at the methodology with which the (old) Commission treated countries in its reviews reveals fundamental flaws and misjudgements. While the general assessment of the Commission points in the right direction, since it considers unit labour costs and other measures of competitiveness, the interpretation of the data is biased by the neoliberal approach the old Commission has never dismissed.[1] The result was to produce misleading recommendations for policy makers at the national level. While it might have been expected that the Commission would not uphold its putative role as honest broker for smaller countries, it is remarkable that a non-partisan approach was missing even for main players of the EMU, i.e., France and Germany.

The French economy was analysed by the Commission in April 2013 and the authors found deeply rooted problems, including a huge

---

1   See European Commission, 2013a.

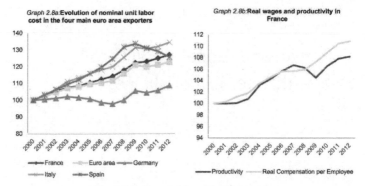

Fig. 8: Net financial flows[1] in Germany[2]

Notes
1 Net debt position of a business sector in relation to gross national product; moving three-year averages
2 Western Germany; Germany starting 1991
Sources: Statistiches Budesamt, AMECO, German Federal Ministry of Finance

and rising current account deficit and a lack of profitability for French enterprises, particularly when compared to its main trading partner, Germany.[2] Figure 8 is taken directly from the Commission paper compare nominal unit labour costs in a manner similar to our analysis in previsou chapters; the Commission also adds real wages and productivity for France.

However, the way in which the Commission comments on the huge divergence between Germany and France that has emerged since the inception of the EMU is clear evidence of theoretical bias with danger-ous policy implications. Thus the Report writes:

The losses in market share (of France) over the last decade have coincided with a deterioration of the cost competitiveness position, as measured through the evolution of unit labour cost (ULC) indicator. Since 2000, nominal ULC increased in France at a faster pace compared to that in the Euro area and Germany in particular (see Graph 2.8a) but still not as rapidly as in Italy and Spain, which have also experienced losses in market shares (-18.4% percent from 2006 to 2011 in Italy and -7.6% in

2   See, European Commission, 2013b.

Spain). While the rise in nominal ULC deteriorated cost competitiveness, the previous IDR noted that the upward trend in real wages outpaced productivity to the detriment of enterprises' profitability. (see Graph 2.8b)

In short, the Commission interprets the left-hand side of Figure 8 through the lense of 'the lower is the ULC the better'. This is indicative of an approach to economic analysis and policy making that will not allow the Commission to lead the EMU finally out of its crisis. Downward competition of unit labour costs without limit and without some determinate scale is absolutely incompatible with forming a currency union based on the principle that a stable and positive inflation rate is to be achieved by all member countries. A currency union that is formed without an explicit and enforced target rate for inflation is both unviable und useless. The target of 1.9 percent that has been set by the ECB has been clearly violated by a race to the bottom in terms of unit labour costs. It is conceivable that there should have been different targets, but the notion that the rule should be 'the lower the better' is simply absurd in view of the strong relationship between unit labour costs and prices.

Equally appalling, however, is the Commission comment on the right-hand side of Figure 8:

The real compensation of employees (in France) has risen quicker than productivity, particularly in 2009, leading to a rapid increase in nominal ULC. While this situation is common to many EU member states, it is in stark contrast with that of Germany, where real wages stagnated or deflated between 2000 and 2007, resulting in a downward pressure on ULC. While it affected the revenues of workers, impacting on living standards and contributing to sluggish domestic consumption, the decreasing labour costs made it possible for German enterprises to simultaneously improve their margins and reduce their prices in order to gain market shares.

For the Commission to state that stagnant or deflating real wages in Germany have led to lower consumption, but at the same time to stress that they have had a beneficial effect on exports is more than nonsense – *it is a monstrous error*. The EU Commission, there can be no doubt, is overseeing what is effectively a large closed economy. To argue that, for a large closed economy, a measure such as wage moderation could be useful despite dampening domestic demand, has to be plain gobbledegook. If the sentence above was rewritten for the world as a whole, it would have been obvious nonsense. For a large closed economy, as well as for the world as a whole, the gain in market share can never make good the loss in domestic demand, given the weight of domestic demand relative to external trade.

It is shown below that moderation in wage growth in Germany has significantly weakened domestic demand in Germany and even dampened investment. Transposing the German model to the European Union as a whole, or the monetary union, would involve grave errors. Indeed, productivity growth without demand growth is the main reason for the world economy as a whole stalling. To recommend the same recipe for Europe that is still in recession is, to put it mildly, deeply irresponsible. To avoid increasing unemployment in line with rising productivity, it is necessary to raise nominal and real incomes, including those of workers.

The In-Depth Report of the Commission is a disappointing document since it fails to deliver what is expected of the guardian of the union treaties and the most singular European institution. In the light of this document it is hard to believe that any country would be fairly treated and that a Commission with such a record could discipline a large country such as Germany.

Indeed, the German IDR published in March 2014 fully supports that disappointing conclusion.[3] Across more than one hundred pages, the Commission attempts to find out whether Germany could be accused of any wrongdoing concerning its huge and persistent current account surplus. Yet, the report on Germany is characterised by confusion. The authors have no way of explaining Germany's trade success since they become entangled in the savings conundrum, discussed in the following pages of this book. In short, the Commission seems unable fully to abandon its dogmatic neoliberal view although it appears to realise that this view does not fit the evidence and results in systematic error.

Thus, in the executive summary the IDR states:

> Persistent very large current account surpluses often reflect subdued domestic demand dynamics. A country with a current account surplus

---

3   See European Commission, 2014a.

transfers consumption from today to tomorrow by investing abroad. In turn, a country with a current account deficit can increase its investment or consumption today but must transfer future income abroad to redeem the external debt. The accumulation of moderate surpluses is a welcome development given the need for saving part of current income to cope with the challenge raised by the demographic outlook, and provide savings to be invested abroad. To the extent that the high surpluses result from large domestic investment gaps, they also hamper the medium- to long-term economic outlook.

And, a few lines later:

Germany is experiencing *macroeconomic imbalances, which require monitoring and policy action*. In particular, the current account has persistently recorded a very high surplus, which reflects strong competitiveness while a large amount of savings were invested abroad. It is also a sign that domestic growth has remained subdued and economic resources may not have been allocated efficiently. Although the current account surpluses do not raise risks similar to large deficits, the size and persistence of the current account surplus in Germany deserve close attention. The need for action so as to reduce the risk of adverse effects on the functioning of the domestic economy and of the Euro area is particularly important given the size of the German economy.

These two contradictory statements imply that the Commission is hovering between two different approaches. On the one hand, the Commisison is unable to abandon the 'savings ideology' whereby consumption is assumed to be transferred from today to tomorrow by investing it abroad. This view is clearly wrong: Germany has not invested large parts of the capital counterpart of its current account surplus, but it has credited the sale of its products today, not tomorrow. Consumption has been transferred from Germany to other countries, but not investment. On the other hand, the Commission admits the possibility of an investment gap in Germany that would hamper the medium-term outlook of the country. That immediately raises the question of how a country with very high investment abroad could at the same time have an investment gap? Is investment abroad so much worse than investment at home and why? Why would there be, according to the Commisison, a misallocation of resources, if Germans produced wonderful goods for the rest of the world to consume, while also investing there accordingly? More fundamentally, why is it necessary to improve competitiveness by cutting wages, if the purpose of the exercise is to save more?

The Commission proceeds to reason in a similar way over many pages. Time and again, it is acknowledged that weak domestic demand, linked to weak wage growth, is the reason for the German surplus, but without ever producing a strong policy argument. It is apparent that the Commission is struggling to find a convincing line but is unable to do so because of strong neoliberal prejudices. Small wonder that, already on page 25, a declaration of failure is delivered: 'The underlying economic reasons for the persistently very high surplus remain, however, difficult to explain.' And on page 27 comes the conclusion: 'A model-based analysis supports the view that the saving and investment behaviour of domestic economic agents has been an important determinant of the surge in Germany's current account surplus.' The unexplained is unexplainable but it has something to do with saving and investment. The Commission has found an elegant way of saying precisely nothing.

Nonetheless, the role of unit labour cost is not fully ignored by the Commision:

> Unit labour cost developments have significant explanatory power for Germany's competitiveness towards the rest of the Euro area. ... Within the Euro area ... labour costs are a key driver of prices of goods and services. Hence, the rising gap in nominal unit labour costs compared to other member states before the crisis clearly improved Germany's cost and price competitiveness, also due to wage growth being above productivity in many other countries.

It seems, then, that unit labour costs are an important determinant of competitiveness, but that has more to do with wages in other countries exceeding productivity rather than with wages in Germany falling short of productivity, and a measure applicable to both apparently does not exist. Even this, however, does not hinder the Commission a few pages later from complimenting Germany for its success, calling it an advantage for the EU as a whole.[4]

---

4   Ibid., p. 93.

Overall, the Commission, whose term of office came to an end in 2014, has produced a document that demonstrates confusion and ignorance, creating a bad precedent for its role in future conflicts. The Commission has succumbed to Germany's political and economic power, instead of defending the smaller countries with reasonable arguments. Furthermore, the IDR has revealed the intellectual difficulties faced by the Commission in reviewing the evidence and understanding the complex interaction of nations without falling prey to mainstream prejudices. The Macroeconomic Imbalance Procedure has been accorded enormous weight in the attempt to create better integration following the Eurozone crisis. But, by acting in a partisan and biased way, the Commission up to now has ensured that the entire exercise has been in vain. Whether the new Commission under Jean-Claude Juncker that took over in 2014 will change the approach fundamentally remains to be seen. The fact that confusion on that matter prevails at the global scale and among academics too bodes badly for a fundamental shift in the Commissions work.

⊠. THE GLOBAL POLITICAL FAILURE TO AVOID EXTERNAL IMBALANCES

It was previously mentioned that current account imbalances per se should not be the main focus of economic policy given the difficulties in quantifying appropriate limits beyond that imbalances would be truly unsustainable, not to mention all the circumstances under which exceptions might be tolerated. There are several good reasons why a current account may be in deficit or surplus at any given point in time. The domestic economy, for instance, may be growing faster than its trade partners, causing imports to rise more than exports (e.g. the United States in the 1990s). Another reason might be that a country could be a major importer of a commodity whose price is on an upward trend, thus increasing the import bill without any compensation through higher exports (e.g. the group of 'low-income, food deficit countries'). A still further reason could be that a country may serve as a hub for foreign enterprises to produce manufactures on a large scale, but may not yet have enough high-income layers of the population to consume the level of imports that would equilibrate exports (e.g. China).

In all such cases, a short-term buffer of net capital inflows or outflows would be needed to allow for the smooth functioning of the international trading system. In other words, deficits or surpluses on the current account would not in themselves be indicative of a systemic problem that demanded coordinated intervention. Moreover, what would matter above all would not be so much the current account position of any single country – some commodity exporters, for instance, could expect to maintain their surpluses indefinitely (eg. Saudi Arabia). What would truly matter would be a loss of competitiveness in the aggregate that may be at the origin of a current account deficit.

The only current account imbalances that are clearly unsustainable are those originating from a loss of competitiveness for the economy as a whole, which would be reflected in an appreciation of the real exchange rate. A general overvaluation of a country's currency would mean that the nominal exchange rate of its currency would have appreciated against other currencies by more than would be warranted in terms of the difference between the domestic price level and unit labour costs.

The fact that exchange rates play a pivotal role in this respect is supported by abundant empirical evidence relating to the factors influencing current account reversals. UNCTAD's Trade and Development Report 2008, for instance, showed that, rather than being driven by autonomous savings and investment decisions of domestic and foreign agents, current account reversals tend to be driven by external shocks emerging from both goods markets and financial markets. In particular, improvements in the current account were usually accompanied either by positive terms-of-trade shocks (a real exchange rate depreciation) or by a panic in the international capital markets followed by sudden stops in capital flows.

The deeper reason why international policy makers are unable to deal with current account deficits and surpluses adequately is a fallacy of composition. Countries becoming indebted against their trading partners over extended periods sooner or later face the issue of the sustainability of that debt and of their ability to service the debt and to repay the principal. However, repayment among countries always involves the willingness of the creditor to change position and become a net debtor from being a net creditor. Among individuals, it might be possible for a debtor to turn his or her position from debtor to creditor reducing consumption, or somehow increasing the inflow of income without ever involving the activities of the creditor. But this is not possible in most cases where creditors and debtors are countries. If the creditor country defended its position by all means, it would be very difficult, or even impossible, for the debtor country to reverse the situation.

This is the well-known 'transfer problem', which Keynes analysed in connection with the Treaty of Versailles following the First World War in his famous book 'The Economic Consequences of the Peace'. He came to the striking conclusion that Germany, having been forced to pay enormous war reparations, would need in the end to build current account surpluses over an extended period, and would have to gain market shares at the expense of the allies, if it were ever to become able to pay. If the Allies refused to give Germany that room of economic manoeuvre, the payment of the reparations would be simply impossible.

It is tragic that Germany, the victim of Allied conditionality at that time, fails to understand its current relationship with the peripheral members of the EMU. Germany insists on the position that 'everybody has to improve competitiveness' and – at the same time – defends its international market share.[5] Thus, Germany is directly preventing a solution of the Eurozone crisis by creating a 'transfer problem'. Competitiveness is a relative concept and current accounts must be balanced for the Eurozone as a whole since the rest of the world would not accept current account surpluses from such a huge block of countries and could enforce its position through exchange rate manipulation. Hence, the German approach violates fundamental economic logic. This, however, is partly due to the inability of the mainstream in economics to provide the material necessary for a sound approach.

⊠. THE FAILURE OF MAINSTREAM THEORY TO EXPLAIN TRADE IMBALANCES

It is worth stressing at this point that the analysis and policy recommendations typically produced by the IMF, the European Commission and other international bodies suffer from these fundamental theoretical flaws. In particular, conclusions drawn about the world based on an identity such as the ex post equality of savings to investment are generally useless. It means nothing to examine an economy that had an external imbalance discovering that – according to standard bookkeeping rules – no country could run a current account deficit that was not financed by (the net 'savings' of) other countries.

The identity of savings and investment is totally silent both on causality and on the mechanisms that bring it about. Causation and the

---

5   See Merkel, 2013, and Schäuble, 2011.

theoretical links between the behaviour of economic agents at home and abroad would have to be introduced before policy conclusions could be drawn successfully. The traditional conjecture of neoliberal theory that savings lead and investment follows is simply not tenable. It is enough to consider that at present most of the poorer countries in the world are surplus countries. Are the surpluses of poor countries the result of a surplus of savings in the proper sense of the word, or have they resulted from plain fear of confronting current account deficits again, given the extremely painful experience of financial crises and creditor 'conditionality' in the 1980s and 1990s?

Even a sophisticated and liberal (in the American sense) economist such as Paul Krugman has fallen victim to the fallacy of deploying bookkeeping as a theory in foreign trade and international transactions. Some time ago, in response to the claim by the new Nobel Prize winner, Eugene Fama, that higher savings would lead to higher investment, Krugman did a great job in clarifying the role of accounting identities in economic analysis.[6]

He wrote: 'The immediate thing Fama should have asked himself, even if completely ignorant of the history of macroeconomics, is why the causation necessarily runs from savings to investment. Why not the other way around?' Alas, this is exactly the question that Krugman should have asked himself in connection with the other accounting identity, the one that states that foreign savings always equal the domestic current account deficit. For, he has fallen victim to this identity in his own work and policy recommendations.

In the above mentioned case of the domestic deficit, Krugman is on solid ground by stressing the dynamics of overall income in the case when consumers decide to save more. If consumers cut spending in an attempt to save more, investors would face declining utilisation of capacity, or the involuntary accumulation of inventories, and would thus cut rather than increase investment. Krugman concludes that:

> consumers may find that they're not saving as much as they intended to, because their incomes fall. Naturally, these unintended results will lead to further changes in behaviour, with enterprises cutting production and consumers further reducing spending, until we eventually reach a sort of equilibrium in which desired saving and desired investment match

---

6   See Krugman, 2013a.

up; this new equilibrium need not be one in which investment rises, and could well be one in which investment falls.

Krugman's more general conclusion is also right:

The point, in any case, is that accounting identities can only tell you so much. Anyone who claims that the identities tell you everything you know, without an actual model of how things work, is just doing bad economics.

However, when it comes to external savings and their accounting counterpart, that fundamental point appears to escape him.[7] In response to the German critique of the Treasury attack on the German current account surplus, Krugman wrote:

It is a basic accounting identity that
        Current account = Savings – Investment
    Any story about the determination of the current account balance must take this identity into account. … So while it's impressive that Germany can run a surplus despite quite high labour costs, and that's a testimony to the quality of its stuff, ultimately the surplus reflects high savings relative to investment.

In this instance, Krugman appears to have missed a fundamental relationship in the external dynamics of modern economies. This is not new, however. Already in 1992, Krugman had stated that:[8]

An external deficit must have as its counterpart an excess of domestic investment over domestic savings, which makes it natural to look for sources of a deficit in an autonomous change in the national savings rate.

As has been noted in response:[9]

suggesting that the identity implies causality and giving 'saving' a specific, namely a leading role in the process, is unjustified. The fact that – from an

---

7   See Krugman, 2013b.
8   See Krugman, 1992, p. 5.
9   UNCTAD, Trade and Development Report 2006, annex A to Chapter 1.

ex-post point of view – a gap has emerged between saving and investment in one country does not hint at an 'autonomous' decision of any economic agent in any of the involved countries. The plans of one group of actors cannot be realised without taking into account a highly complex interaction of these plans with those of other actors, as well as price and quantity changes under conditions of objective uncertainty about the future. In order to give the savings-investment identity informational content, it is necessary to identify the variables that determine the movements of each, saving, consumption and investment, and in consequence the national income of the country, along with the national incomes of all its trading partners.

In a non-stationary environment, any increase in expenditure (increase in a net debt position of one sector) raises profits and any increase in saving (net creditor position) reduces profits. Whether saving or investment change here or there, whether the beneficiaries (or losers) of the adjustment process are located in the country where the shock originated or in other countries, does not change the course of events. The decision of a certain group of economic agents (private or public, domestic or foreign) to spend less out of their current income diminishes profits. A drop in foreign savings (a falling current account deficit) can actually mean higher domestic profits and more investment instead of a drop in investment.

A current account deficit, or a growing 'inflow of foreign saving', very often emerges as the result of falling terms of trade, or a lasting real exchange rate appreciation. Rising oil prices, for example, induced by rising demand in a large new consumer country, such as China, would increase the oil bill of the industrialised consumer countries. This would mean rising demand (in nominal terms) for oil as the demand elasticity would be very low in the short run. A current account deficit in the consumer countries would emerge and the higher oil bill would be financed by the international banking system. Financing would be made easier by the fact that the banks would expect the oil exporting countries to recycle their additional revenues quickly towards the consumer countries. But the origin of these 'foreign savings' would clearly not have been the decision of the private households in the oil producing countries to save more than before.

A real appreciation of the domestic currency would normally induce consumers to buy more foreign products and to reduce consumption of broadly similar domestic products. If the trading part-ner's banking system was willing and able to finance the resulting gap between imports and exports (which would simply be a consumer credit to foreign clients), domestic income would fall as the revenues and the profits (the savings) of domestic enterprises would fall (while profits would rise in the depreciating country). In this case, once again, the accounting identity would indicate an increase of foreign savings without even a single private household having taken the autonomous decision to save more than before.

Thus, if a member of a currency union, such as Germany, decided to exert political pressure to lower domestic wages in an attempt to improve competitiveness, the first thing that would happen (as a result of this process that would be equivalent to a real depreciation) would be a fall in relative prices and the replacement of some domestic prod-ucts by German products in the trading partners' markets. The other members of the currency union would experience a real appreciation and their domestic enterprises would face a loss of competitiveness. The domestic banks in the deficit countries would be willing to finance the rising current account gap as long as they could count on refinancing through the ECB for transactions within the currency union.

Yet, nothing would have happened to savings proper in Germany. Neither the private nor the public sector would have changed its behav-iour. German enterprises, taking advantage of the fall in wages, would be making higher profits in foreign transactions than before, and foreign enterprises less. At the same time, a current account surplus would emerge in Germany, which, in the terms of the accounting iden-tity, could be interpreted as Germany saving more than before.

Attempting to explain the Eurozone crisis through the capital flow hypothesis is fundamentally flawed. Namely, it is a fallacious idea that Germany had a savings glut and German savings were needed in Spain, Italy or even France to build houses and hotels. Moreover, to explain the huge German current account surplus it is by no means sufficient to argue that low interest rates in Germany induced German savers to invest abroad. In fact, interest rates in the relevant nominal terms across the Eurozone were exactly at the same level as in Germany. In real terms, interest rates were actually lower in the periphery because prices and wages there were on a higher growth trajectory than in Germany.

⊠. THE NEOLIBERAL APPROACH TO SAVINGS IS GENERALLY FLAWED

The general weakness of the mainstream approach to savings, which is also the approach that the European Commission still seems to adhere to, is evident when it comes to dealing with concrete changes in the behaviour of economic agents. If, for example, the saving rate of households, or of the public sector, or even of other countries (such as oil exporters) suddenly rose, enterprises would be faced with falling demand and falling profits, and would thus react by reducing their investment. Under these conditions, the 'rational expectations' branch of neoliberal theory would assume that enterprises could expect growth to accelerate as a result of the rise in savings. Thus, enterprises would increase their investment expenditure *despite the fact* that demand would be falling, perhaps by switching the financing of the increased investment away from equity (cash flow and profits) towards interest-bearing loans. The mechanism behind this transition would be a fall in interest rates as a result of higher savings.

The implications of this argument are quite perplexing. It is true that, after a fall in demand, enterprises could potentially obtain the same level of profit as they would have done if consumption was unchanged. But, for that, they would have to increase their investment by exactly the amount that is being saved instead of being used for consumption expenditure. And they would be expected to do this even though demand for their products would have dropped. The implication is that enterprises would demand interest-bearing credit to fill the profit gap opened by the decrease in consumption.

In other words, the investing enterprises would increase their borrowing from the financial system by exactly the same amount that they would have acquired 'for nothing' if households continued to spend as much as before. Yet, even if interest rates approached zero, it is evident that the funds that enterprises would need to protect their profits would now be more expensive than before. In short, mainstream economic theory essentially assumes that enterprises would invest more than before despite having to pile up unsold inventory and/or reduce capacity utilisation, and although the financing of their investment has become more costly.

If the assumption of constant or zero profits would be accepted *a priori* the system's dynamics could be accounted for in terms of private consumption smoothing over time. Enterprises would passively adjust to any decision by households, without endangering the equilibrium values of the model, or its inherent stability. Such an economy would be exclusively driven by autonomous consumer decisions, since the model basically assumes totally reactive entrepreneurs, who never take into account actual business conditions when deciding on investment. As a rule, the deterioration of their business in the present is taken as proof of a warranted (expected) improvement in the future. The entire notion is not far off absurdity, but it reflects exactly what the creditor countries in the Eurozone, led by Germany, have been preaching.[10]

Policy makers relying on this kind of thinking typically fail to understand that it simply does not capture key factors of economic life. Above all, it does not capture the time factor and, closely related to it, the availability of information that matters for the sequence of decisions taken by economic agents under uncertainty about the future. In a world of money and uncertainty, the decision to save more and to consume less has grave repercussions on the goods market before it could impact the financial system. But, even considering the possible reaction of the financial system, the decision 'not to have dinner today' depresses the business of preparing dinner today without immediately stimulating any other business, as Keynes argued.[11]

In a world of uncertainty and flexible profits, the intention of individuals to save an absolutely higher sum than before may completely fail because the future income they would realise at the end of the period may be lower than the income they expected to have at the beginning of the period. Even if households succeeded in raising the *share* of savings in their actual income (the savings rate), the *absolute* amount of income saved (and invested) may still be lower, as the denominator of the saving rate (i.e., real income) may have fallen due to the decline in demand and profits, with an induced fall in investment.

The implications for economic policy of the difference between Keynesian and neoliberal theory on savings are tremendous. If either the level or the growth rate of real income is not given and constant, then the implications of the opening of markets and of policy interventions are of overwhelming importance. The neoliberal fixed-profits model does not leave much room for manoeuvre for economic policy. When it considers economic policy options, these tend to be the direct

---

10   See Schäuble, 2011.

11   See Keynes, 1936, p.210.

opposite of those put forward under the Keynesian flexible-profits model. For policy makers who receive recommendations it is of vital interest to know the model on the basis of which these were formed.

If income growth is the main goal of economic policy, then economic policy should clearly focus on ensuring that investment plans would regularly exceed saving plans due to the flexibility of profits. In such a world, even if the private incentive for 'thrift' was unchanged, the economy as a whole would still expand vigorously. The 'savings' corresponding to increased investment would be generated by the investment itself, and the latter would be 'financed' through liquidity created by bank credit based on expansionary monetary policy. Increased investment would stimulate higher profits as temporary monopoly rents would emerge in the corporate sector.

These profits would supply the macroeconomic saving that would be required from an ex post point of view to 'finance' the additional investment. In the flexible-profit approach:

> the departure of profits from zero is the mainspring of change in the ... modern world ... It is by altering the rate of profits in particular directions that entrepreneurs can be induced to produce this rather than that, and it is by altering the rate of profits in general that they can be induced to modify the average of their offers of remuneration to the factors of production.[12]

Moreover, something that is often forgotten in the debates between the advocates of the two approaches is that the adjustment of saving to investment in practice is overlaid by various kinds of exogenous shocks. Interest rates, for example, might not fall if monetary policy is obliged to confront a higher price level stemming from a negative supply shock, or from the depreciation of the national currency – Turkey's attempt to prevent a depreciation of the Lira in January 2014 is a good example. Interest rates may even go up in a cyclical downturn, if financial markets dictate higher interest rates to a small country. The negative effects of falling private demand on profits, finally, might even be aggravated by pro-cyclical fiscal policy if 'austerity' was erroneously seen as a solution.

---

12   See Keynes, 1936, p. 140.

CHAPTER 6

The EMU Heads to Disaster

⊠. EMERGING EUROPEAN MONETARY DISUNION

At the beginning of 2014, unemployment in the EU stood at more than 12 percent. In Spain and Greece, unemployment exceeded 25 percent, while youth unemployment was above an extraordinary 55 percent. More than anything else these figures show the failure of the EU to tackle the problem that has emerged as the 'Eurozone crisis'. Indeed, while the dramatic drop in growth and employment was first caused by the global crisis of 2007–9, after 2010 the debtor nations of the EMU were deprived of the means of fighting the recession and were forced to adopt pro-cyclical policies of a scale that was last seen in the 1930s.

The German mantra of 'austerity as the only solution' was applied to all countries that were forced to ask for help when their access to the global capital markets ceased, or was blocked de facto by very high interest rates.[1] Once again, obsession with apparent fiscal problems dominated the debate and the conditions that were demanded by the troika and the Eurogroup to open the coffers of the creditor nations focused on consolidating the public budgets of deficit countries at any price and as quickly as possible.

With German dominance over export markets persisting and given Germany's refusal to adjust its own economic model the future looks bleak for the Eurozone. The lack of policy instruments to tackle the recession, the conditionality attached to the adjustment programmes imposed on the crisis economies, the dysfunctional 'structural' adjustment itself and the prospect of looming deflation have raised the costs of remaining within the EMU up to the point where political upheaval on the right threatens democracy and the EU. Failure to address the rate of unemployment and rising poverty has paved the way for radical right-wing and populist anti-European parties in creditor as

---

1 See Schäuble, 2011.

well as in debtor countries. Against this danger, the benefits of being a member of the EMU are small and, more importantly, they are shrinking fast.

The disintegration of the capital markets in the EMU following the financial crisis has drastically reduced the benefits of belonging to the monetary union and accepting a common monetary policy. Nearly five years after the outbreak of the Eurozone crisis things have not changed significantly. The return of Ireland, Spain and Greece to the capital markets came at an incredibly high price, the countries having had to pay a very high rate of interest on their bonds considering that they were in recession and deflation. But even worse has been the historically unprecedented costs of the adjustment that they have had to accept to reach that point. Furthermore, the limited ability to raise funds in the capital market has not removed the constraints on domestic economic policy. For Greece, in particular, and as is shown in detail in the last chapter of this book, neither fiscal policy nor any other normal economic tool is available to stimulate an economy that has gone through a great depression. At the same time, monetary conditions (interest rates and real exchange rates) are clearly worse in the deficit than in the surplus countries. Record low interest rates on government bonds in the surplus countries have laid the ground for easy consolidation of their budgets, while benign monetary conditions might begin to stimulate their economies.

For the EMU as a whole, applying 'structural reforms' simultaneously to the labour markets of several countries has entailed a dramatic drop in domestic demand, and contributed to a collapse of trade flows. The effect of wage cutting in countries where domestic demand strongly exceeds foreign demand (in France, Italy, Portugal and Spain domestic demand amounts to three-quarters of total demand; by contrast, in Ireland the export share of GDP is more than 100 percent) has directly reduced aggregate demand. In this way, the imposed wage cuts have directly increased unemployment rather than, as the troika expected, reducing it.

Consequently, there has been a remarkably strong correlation between the adjustment demanded by the troika and economic decline in peripheral EMU countries. The more closely countries have followed the troika prescription, the more their economies have shrunk and even collapsed. France and Italy have experienced a strong deceleration of growth even with unchanged wage growth (and growth in ULC). But all countries that have actually undergone the troika 'treatment' since 2010 have faced stunning decline.

Paradoxically, those countries that have gone quite a way toward improving their competitiveness by reducing wages offer the final proof that this is exactly the wrong way to proceed. Indeed it is even worse than that: the brutal logic of the adjustment imposed on some smaller countries has meant that the others, including France and Italy, could not apply it without risking major political destabilisation. If France and Italy went the way of the troika, it is almost certain that the entire Eurozone would be thrown into depression resulting in a sharp drop of prices and long-lasting deflation.

It is hard to imagine that the democratic regimes in these countries would survive such an event. It is even likely that radical parties of the Right would become dominant by campaigning against Europe and the Euro. On the other hand, if France and Italy do not adjust, their economies would be destroyed in terms of competitiveness making it impossible to prosper on the basis of balanced trade. Their deficits on current account would keep on growing putting their entire economic edifice in jeopardy. But then, if France and Italy do not apply the troika adjustment programme and Germany does not change its stance, the end of the Euro as a common currency would be only a question of time.

In short, the accumulated divergences during the first years of the EMU and the terrible nature of the adjustment programmes have put the very survival of the EU in question. And yet, European policy makers appear to be oblivious to this fact. They are even less willing to engage in a policy effort to turn around the overall economy and to stop the growing divergences within the EMU. The prospect of disintegration and eventual collapse of the European Union can no longer be ignored.

ⅺ. Neither a Political Union Nor a Transfer Union are Plausible Solutions for the EMU

Several normally realistic people – even within the Left – still dream of a fully politically unified Europe that would help overcome the difficulties currently faced by EMU. There is little doubt that this is just a dream that should not be allowed to guide political action. Its key weakness is that there is no European 'demos' that could support the functioning of political union across Europe. And nor is there any realistic prospect of such a 'demos' emerging in the foreseeable future. Indeed, the democratic rights of the European people would be severely compromised by any further attempts to bypass the nation states of Europe in the hope of creating a European 'superstate', or a political union. The performance of the EU machinery in the course of the crisis, often by passing the democratic process in the member states of the EMU, and even helping appoint unelected prime ministers in Italy and Greece, is a sobering omen.

In point of fact, the obvious inability and unwillingness to discuss honestly the reasons of the failure of the EMU during the last five years demonstrates how divided European countries really are. To believe that the same countries, with the same political systems, could create a commonly held perception across Europe that genuine political union is the way forward and, moreover, that this perception could be translated into enhanced democratic practice, is plain silly. Current experience indicates that, given the obvious inability of European institutions to manage a complex system like the EMU appropriately, the currency union was too ambitious a goal. The implicit attempt to advance more rapidly towards political union by first forming a currency union has largely failed, leaving Europe in a worse state than before. Paradoxically, if Europe is to progress again, it first has to retreat.

At the core of the failure of EMU lies the German economic model. Other European countries have been unable to question the German model openly and to convince Germany that it is not even in its own interest to opt for competition rather than cooperation of nations, particularly among the members of the currency union. Germany has emerged as the dominant power of the EU, dictating terms to others, crucially influencing policy debates at the level of the EU, and jealously guarding its advantages. Acknowledging that lack of cooperation will be a fact of life for the foreseeable future would be a necessary first step towards reshaping the institutional arrangements that are required for a peaceful division of labour in Europe.

Without a currency union, it would again become possible to use currency devaluation as an instrument of economic policy and thus to fend off attempts by some countries economically to occupy others. Devaluation has indeed been the most frequently used mechanism in modern history to respond to the behaviour of an aggressive trading partner without engaging in outright protectionism. A system of orderly devaluations (and revaluations on the other side) might preserve the core idea on which economic integration in Europe has been founded, namely that relatively free trade is better than autarchy.

Finally, forming a transfer union to support the EMU would be neither a feasible, nor a desirable step among independent and sovereign nations. Even in Germany – a single country, with the same language and the same history – the transfer union that was put in place to confront the problems created by the German Monetary Union of West and East Germany has failed to deliver harmonious coexistence of the two constituent parts and has frequently provoked political tensions. There is no member state of the EU whose people would accept becoming dependent on German transfers as a way of consolidating the existing economic imbalances and in order to avoid relying on the capital markets. Equivalently, Germany and other surplus countries already face enormous difficulties (objective and subjective) to persuade their citizens temporarily to finance presumably 'lazy Southerners', and right-wing parties are able to exploit the festering tensions. Institutionalising a system of fiscal transfers to deal with budget and/or current account imbalances in the EMU would be a recipe for profound nationalist friction in the future.

CHAPTER 7

What Could and Should Be Done by the Left?

⬚. A CONFUSED RESPONSE SO FAR

If the response of the European authorities to the Eurozone crisis has been appalling, the response by the European Left to the challenge thrown by the turmoil and by the conservative hardening of the EMU has not exactly been impressive. The Left has generally lagged behind events and failed to capitalise on the most profound crisis of European capitalism since the second World War. With regard to the boldness of its ideas, it has often trailed the Right, and even the extreme Right. Characteristic of the Left has been its inability to put together a persuasive economic programme that could resolve the crisis and lead to growth, while improving the condition of working people.

To be fair, the political Left has certainly offered sharp critiques of austerity, liberalisation and privatisation; it has shown the emptiness of neoliberal economics; it has decried falling wages as the answer to unemployment; it has advocated financial controls and public investment. But it has also failed to put these ideas into a coherent whole that could provide a persuasive answer to the crisis. A major reason for this failure has been the unwillingness of the bulk of the European Left to confront directly the vexed issue of the common currency but also the nature of the EU as that has evolved in recent decades.

During the last couple of years, nevertheless, things have begun to change in the periphery of the Eurozone, primarily in Greece and Spain. The depth and the breadth of the crisis have been unprecedented, and the Left has emerged as the major beneficiary of the political turbulence. The prospect of a radical government based on the Left in the near future is very real in Greece, a development that could catalyse profound political and social developments across Europe. The problem is, however, that the Greek Left has not yet put together a persuasive and coherent programme for the economy, society and polity. The threat of failure hangs large over the enterprise.

The Greek Left has benefitted greatly from the collapse of the legitimacy of all political forces that have supported the troika bailouts and the attendant austerity policies imposed on the country since the start of the crisis in 2010. However, its own positive proposals to deal with the crisis and to reshape Greek economy and society have not been nearly as effective. The Greek Left, as many others, still largely refuses to acknowledge the nature of the Eurozone crisis, and believes that it could be resolved without any major social rupture, and even without challenging Greece's integration in the EU and the EMU. Essentially, it is preparing for government in the charmed belief that the crisis could be confronted be relaxing fiscal policy and implementing income and wealth redistribution. This remains a fundamental weakness in view of the real tasks that a Left government in Greece would have to deal with, and given the role that it could play in changing the political outlook of the rest of Europe.

The task for the Left in Europe is to develop the outline of a plan capable of dealing with the Eurozone crisis primarily in the peripheral but also in the core countries of the EMU. The plan, analysed and detailed in the last chapter of this book for the case of Greece, is directly relevant to other peripheral countries caught in the current policy trap. It is not a complete programme, of course, since forming such a programme would require a coordinated and large-scale effort involving several social actors. Nonetheless, it is a programmatic statement that incorporates substantial research and sketches answers for the systemic crisis of Greek capitalism and perhaps other peripheral countries of the Eurozone.

Finally, a broader objective of the plan would be to outline some necessary and fundamental steps, if European societies are to move in the direction of growth with social justice, thus shifting the balance of class forces in favour of labour and channelling social development in a new direction. Achieving these objectives would require confronting directly the institutions of the EU and in particular the failed mechanisms of the EMU. More broadly, it would require adopting a clear social perspective that would confront directly the utterly dysfunctional capitalism of our age.

◻. STRIVING FOR AN ALTERNATIVE PATH WITHIN THE CURRENT EMU: AN 'IMPOSSIBLE TRIAD'

An alternative programme in a peripheral country based on new economics and politics and implemented by a government of the Left would certainly lead to conflict with the institutions and mechanisms of the EMU and the EU. It is important to lay out in this section the fundamental reasons for such conflict, which might be summed up as 'the impossible triad' faced by a peripheral country within the EMU. Conflict is likely to focus, first, on the problem of restructuring debt and, second, on the more general issue of lifting austerity and taking the necessary steps to rebalance peripheral economies in the direction of growth and equality. Opposition from the neoliberal consensus and from the established interests at the heart of the EU that have coalesced around the EMU is likely to be relentless.

It is important in this context to bear in mind that bailout agreements have included loan facility agreements that were well supported legally as well as Memoranda of Understanding on 'conditionality' that the recipient country was legally obliged to follow. The austerity policies undertaken by Greece since 2010, for instance, have been dictated by a legal and institutional framework that is mainly aimed at protecting the interests of lenders and enforcing the continued servicing of the national debt. More broadly, the conservative restructuring of the EMU, undertaken at the behest of Germany since 2010, has hardened the legal and institutional framework of the EMU and the EU with regard to both austerity and liberalisation, as was discussed in previous chapters. Consequently, any action by a Left government that would seek to implement an alternative programme by dealing with public debt, or lifting austerity measures, would directly challenge the entire framework of the EMU and the EU. There can be no compartmentalisation of policy measures, or initiatives in this regard.

It follows that a Left government in a peripheral country ought to be prepared to enter conflict with the EU across the entire field of adjustment policies. After all, the expectation among EU bureaucrats is that policies agreed by governments in crisis countries during 2010–14 would continue to be followed. By this token, a Left government would have to take unilateral action on several issues, if it wished to change the direction of its country.

It cannot be overemphasised that without effective debt restructuring a Left government in a peripheral country would find it impossible to implement an alternative programme, even in the short run. To be sure, there would be some room for fiscal manoeuvre during the initial period, particularly on issues related to ameliorating the conditions of those who have been worst hit by the crisis. But no sustainable change in policy would be possible without dealing with debt, and thus without facing conflict across the entire framework of policy that has been put in place during the last few years by the EU. The implication is that conflict would inevitably follow.

To be more specific, debt restructuring in peripheral countries would involve losses for both private and official lenders, though the relative weight of each would differ from country to country. Losses for private lenders would obviously entail losses for the banking system that would have to be confronted in part through provision of public funds, if they are not to cause a banking collapse. Furthermore, there would be losses for pension and insurance funds that would also have to be managed in part through public intervention. Losses for official lenders, on the other hand, would imply direct losses for the taxpayers/ voters of EU and other countries.

Debt restructuring for the periphery, in short, would entail costs for core countries, whether these would be the cost of shoring up banks and pension funds, or the cost of writing off loans made entirely out of public funds. For the restructuring to be consensual, it would be necessary to secure the approval of several European political systems, something that would require a complex political process of weighing losses and benefits. In all probability, there would be a collapse of consensus, and conflict would emerge. But even in the unlikely event of a consensual debt write-off, accepted by the political systems of core countries, there is little doubt that the EU would at the same time insist on continuing with the policies of fiscal rigidity which are now formally embedded in the structure of the union and which entail monitoring and fines for 'delinquent' countries.

There is, thus, a kind of 'impossible triad' that would be faced by a Left government in the periphery. It is impossible to have all three of the following: first, achieving effective restructuring of the debt; second, abandoning austerity; and third, continuing to operate within the institutional and policy framework of the EU and particularly the EMU. A Left government would be wasting its time and energy – not to mention undermining itself politically – if it attempted to achieve the 'impossible triad'. The real aim ought to be to achieve deep debt write-offs and to change economic policy drastically, while negotiating a new relationship with the EU and the EMU.

☒. Confronting the EU Effectively: Aims and Actions of a Left Government

In view of the preceding analysis, the negotiating stance of a Left government in a peripheral country is a complex issue that requires careful analysis. Conflict across the entire framework of policy would be inevitable for such a government that set its vision on achieving a deep debt write-off and lifting of austerity. But there can be no conflict with the EU on this score that would not also raise the spectre of EMU exit. A Left government should not be scared or cowed by this prospect, but instead make tactical use of EMU membership while engaging in negotiations. Clarity is fundamental on what is possible, bearing in mind the 'impossible triad' as well as placing priority on writing off debt and lifting austerity. A government that drew its strength from its own people ought not to be scared of potential exit from the Eurozone, if it wished to achieve its fundamental aims. Moreover, if it succeeded, it could change Europe in favour of working people in general.

There are two important bargaining chips that the EU would have in the course of confrontation: first, provision of liquidity to banks by the ECB and, second, provision of official lending to the government by a variety of bodies. Both are likely to be used as blackmail tools, as was shown in the case of Cyprus in 2013. Since most peripheral countries, including Greece, have primary budget surpluses, however, official lending to the government has lost much of its earlier importance.

The most powerful lever available to the EU, therefore, would be the interruption of ECB liquidity. Unfortunately there could be no decisive response by a Left government to the liquidity threat within the confines of EMU. This is ultimately the reason why the 'impossible triad' holds. Nonetheless, it is possible to adopt tactics that could create room for negotiation, thus strengthening the borrower's side and weakening that of the lenders. It is conceivable, for instance, that the national central bank would provide Emergency Liquidity Assistance for a period, even in the face of opposition by the Eurosystem. Similar tactics would be to declare a bank holiday followed by restrictions in bank operations, while appointing a Public Commissioner for the financial system. Finally, the government of the Left could impose capital controls.

It is worth stressing that taking these measures is perfectly plausible within the confines of the EMU, and indeed the EU has itself deployed them at various times in the course of the crisis, particularly in the context of the Cyprus crisis in 2013, with the exception of appointing a Public Commissioner for finance. Their adoption would demonstrate the determination of a Left government to achieve its primary aims, thus allowing for more effective confrontation with the EU. They would also be important to forestalling the emergence of a massive crisis that could potentially result in a bank run.

Such measures would also be useful in preparing the ground for exit from the EMU, if the country was eventually forced in that direction. It ought to be restated, nonetheless, that these measures could not decisively solve the problem of liquidity as long as the country remained in the EMU. The only real solution for that would be to create capacity to generate liquidity autonomously, which would mean introducing a new national currency. It is of great importance for a Left government to be clear on this score.

Consequently, a Left government should take steps from the very beginning to re-establish the independence of the national central bank from the Eurosystem. This would mean re-creating institutional capacity to generate liquidity in the national currency as well as monitoring capital controls and managing exchange rates. These are difficult tasks and the skills in delivering them have declined in all peripheral countries. It is likely that experienced people formerly in the public service would have to be recalled from retirement as well as experts invited from abroad.

Furthermore, a Left government should take immediate steps to create alternative forms of liquidity for the public to use, even if these were still denominated in Euro. As we know from the experience of Cyprus in 2013, bank restrictions would make public access to cash very difficult. There is also likely to be substantial hoarding of Euro-denominated banknotes as the confrontation with the EU would become fiercer. To minimise the effect on the economy, the government could potentially issue short-term paper (scrip), denominated in Euro. The scrip would have forced circulation since the government would declare it acceptable for payments to the public sector, including taxes.

This action would be, in effect, the emergence of a parallel monetary system, even if still in Euro. A Left government should be clear, however, that a parallel monetary system could never be a permanent arrangement but would in practice prove the first step towards issuing a national currency. Scrip could be easily converted into the national currency, if the country were forced out of the Euro.

It is conceivable that these tactics, plus social mobilisation plus some international support (the extent of which must not be exaggerated), would help a new Left government succeed in achieving a deep write-off of debt plus abandonment of austerity. However, the EU is extremely unlikely to consent to these demands without requiring exit from the EMU. A Left government should consider itself extremely successful if it secured a negotiated (non-confrontational) exit of this sort. It is conceivable that the EU would find this prospect acceptable since the 'problem' country would exit – inevitably bearing some costs – thus leaving the rest of the EMU 'healthier'. Exit could be seen as the price paid by Greece, or another peripheral country, for a debt write-off.

If exit was agreed on a non-confrontational basis, there would be several technical ways in which the EU could facilitate it. The legal and technical arguments circulating in 2009–12 and 'proving' that exit from the EMU was impossible, or that it would also inevitably bring exit from the EU, were largely nonsense. Exit is perfectly feasible, particularly if the EU was prepared to facilitate it. After all, the mechanisms of the European Monetary System, the previous system of fixing exchange rates, are still extant, and could be re-activated. More specifically, facilitation could take the form of continued provision of liquidity by the ECB to the banks for a period of, perhaps, six months to a year. Critically, facilitation of exit could take the form of supporting the exchange rate to prevent collapse until the country became capable of defending it itself. An outcome of this nature would be, by far, the optimal solution for peripheral countries and it might also be the least problematic solution for the EU itself.

Given the political and economic interests involved in the EMU, however, it is far more likely that consensual exit would prove impossible. The lenders are unlikely to tolerate, much less to help, a Left government that would have insisted in writing off debt as well as abandoning austerity and turning economic policy into a completely different direction. Consequently, a Left government should be prepared for confrontational exit, which would also be fully feasible, though more costly. The first step in this process would probably be the declaration of default on the debt, which could take a variety of forms but the content would be the same: cessation of payments of interest and capital and a unilateral call for negotiations on what will be paid and how. Settling the issue of debt would of course be a long-drawn-out process that would require popular mobilisation, a Debt Audit and strong legal support.

It cannot be overstressed that the path of confrontational exit requires political legitimacy and active popular support, if it is to be handled successfully by a government on the Left. It is important that the government should make it clear that exit would be forced on it by the EU refusing to accept reasonable terms on writing off debt and lifting austerity. It is also important to obtain open political support by putting the issue squarely to the electorate and the organised labour movement.

Note that confrontational exit could also be managed by a nationalist and authoritarian government, but this would be disastrous for working people because it would involve taking oppressive political measures, and it would probably shift the bulk of the costs on wage labour and the middle class. For a Left government, securing political legitimacy and active popular support for potential EMU exit would be tasks requiring immediate political planning.

CHAPTER 8

Managing Confrontational Exit from the EMU

Confrontational exit would be a difficult process but dealing with it would be perfectly feasible as long as there was sufficient awareness of the likely problems, a degree of preparation and clear popular support. Without clarity among working people and preparedness to deal with the shock and its implications, it would be very difficult for a new government to deal successfully with confrontational exit. If, on the other hand, the issue was well understood and there was no fear of its implications, exit from the EMU could open a path to social transformation in favour of labour. Much would depend on the preparatory actions taken during negotiation.

The concrete problems and the likely steps of exit are no longer a hypothetical issue – light has been cast on them by the intervention of the EU in Cyprus in 2013. A useful way of classifying the problems for purposes of analysis but also to shape policy would be as short- and medium-term. The former include mostly liquidity (money circulation), banking, trade and provisioning of key markets. The latter include fundamentally the restructuring of production that would be necessary in peripheral countries.

To handle a confrontational exit successfully it would be vital to have bank and capital controls already in place as well as circulating Euro-denominated scrip. These measures could be taken in the course of negotiations helping the position of a Left government while also making it easier to handle the implications of exit. By the same token, they would stir popular support and awareness that would be fundamental to dealing with exit. This is the best that could be hoped for in terms of preparatory actions.

The immediate problems that would subsequently emerge would include:

i) Redenominating the balance sheet of the national central bank. Legal advice would be necessary with regard to liabilities to the Eurosystem as well as with regard to ELA. Default for a central bank is a much more complex issue than for a regular bank. The national central bank would have to be recapitalised with newly issued state securities.

ii) Redenominating the balance sheet of commercial banks. Liabilities towards the national central bank could be changed immediately as could deposits and loans contracted under domestic law. Liabilities under foreign law, domestic and international would have to be grouped together, isolated and dealt with gradually. A structure of 'good' and 'bad' banks would have to be created. There would have to be careful auditing of bank debt to avoid saddling the public purse with bad debts.

iii) Redenominating the balance sheet of private enterprises. Debts under foreign law would have to be grouped together and guaranteed by the state, after scrutiny. State support would be necessary.

iv) Redenominating the balance sheet of households. Deposits, mortgages, other debt under domestic law would be redenominated immediately.

v) Redenomination could take place under differential ratios, perhaps depending on the size of deposits or debts, to effect income redistribution and to make the shift more palatable to the popular strata. The simplest solution would, of course, be to use the 1:1 ratio throughout. Use of several ratios would increase complexity, but it would also give the opportunity to effect wealth redistribution.

vi) The needs of monetary circulation could gradually be covered by banks creating liquidity in the new currency. However, during the first period, banknotes in Euro are likely to be hoarded and banknotes in the new currency will take time to produce. Consequently, the circulation of scrip (now denominated in national currency) should be expanded immediately; its value will decline in transactions among third parties, but it will still provide necessary liquidity.

vii) The new currency would be substantially devalued in the international markets. Devaluation would act as a vital lever to recapture the domestic market and to expand exports; but in the short run the results would be negative both for final goods and for inputs. Much would depend on how severe the devaluation would be. The ability to defend the exchange rate would be limited for a significant period of time, and until the balance of trade turned positive. Administrative measures and a range of capital controls would be necessary. It should be stressed, however, that the conditions of most periphery countries in 2014 are vastly different from that in 2010. The current account deficits have shrunk mostly because imports have collapsed due to the destruction of the economy in the course of the recession. The ability to defend the exchange rate, consequently, is markedly greater.

viii) Provisioning of key markets – medicine, food and fuel – would become a significant issue in the short run. Administrative measures would certainly be necessary to secure access to key goods for industry and the most vulnerable social groups. But note that a Left government would in any case need to take strong administrative steps to provide basic goods to those currently being deprived of them, even without exiting the EMU. Moreover, if the current account is practically balanced, the ability to pay for its imports in general is given. Note also that access to fuel, medicine and food have already become deeply problematic for vast layers of working people as a result of the collapse of incomes.

In dealing with the problem it is important to realise that there is currently huge underutilised capacity in the crisis countries in terms of both labour power and means of production in the economy which could be rapidly put to use to provision domestic markets. There is also already significant coverage of key food supplies from domestic sources and a system of prioritising imports to support the most vulnerable groups would not be impossible to establish quickly. In Greece, for example, there is good domestic coverage for energy to produce electricity, and it would be possible to have interstate agreements with sympathetic governments to boost the availability of car fuel. Finally, existing capacity indicates that it would also be possible to deal satisfactorily with the provision of medicines, partly though mobilising domestic resources, and partly through prioritising key imports, including cheaply available generic drugs from a variety of suppliers across the world.

CHAPTER 9

Dismantling the EMU

It is instructive now briefly to turn to the issue of EMU membership for core countries, which are in a different position compared to the periphery. As was already explained in the earlier chapters of this book, the EMU has become a mechanism for recession and for the imposition of neoliberal policies, which affects France and Italy particularly badly. The monetary union offers precious few benefits to the people of Europe, in economic, social and political terms. It is unquestionably a great historical failure as well as being a structure that denies democracy directly and openly, not to mention asserting German economic and political ascendancy and directly limiting national sovereignty. The notion of a 'Europe of the people', or of a form of money that would act as a lever of solidarity, prosperity and convergence has been completely undermined.

In view of the evolution of the EMU and of the political and social forces within it, it is fair to conclude that there is no prospect of reform in a direction that would favour working people and societies as a whole. Proposals to mutualise debt or to make the ECB freely purchase sovereign debt, thus enabling EMU states to borrow more easily, run against the simple fact that they would impose costs on core countries, above all, on Germany. These costs would take the form of higher borrowing rates for the German state as well as the risk of losses in case of default by other sovereign borrowers. Proposals to lift austerity and to adopt expansionary fiscal policy but without first dealing with the problem of debt are not coherent. Proposals to promote a well-funded investment drive across Europe to raise productivity and strengthen peripheral economies invariably run against the problem of securing funding and providing the financial mechanisms that would support the investment projects.

The only viable solution, as has been explained in depth throughout this work, would be dramatically to change the domestic and international policies of Germany, adopting an entirely different approach to wages and to domestic demand. If the EMU acknowledged the importance of managing unit labour costs and inflation in an equitable way among its members, it could potentially become viable. The prospect of this development materialising, however, is pretty close to non-existent.

At bottom, the historic failure of the EMU is due to its very essence: the Euro is not a currency run by a federal or a unitary state that corresponds to a 'demos'. Rather, it is the money of an alliance of unequal sovereign states riven with hierarchical relations with Germany at the top. It has not operated in the interests of all its members, it is currently strangling the economy of Europe, it has sown tensions among European states, it has undermined democratic practice across the continent, and it cannot be reformed in the current political setting. The realistic progressive option would be to return to national currencies, thus facilitating recovery of economic independence, defence of democracy and protection of national sovereignty. Naturally, reintroducing national currencies alone could not deliver these changes but it would be a vital step in that direction. The real difficulty would be to return to national currencies without releasing economic nationalism and introducing competitive devaluations, or relying on market forces to determine exchange rates.

The most complex technical problem would be finding a viable new foreign exchange regime. The new currency of deficit countries could, for instance, be introduced at an administrative rate of 1:1 to the Euro, but it would obviously depreciate rapidly in the foreign exchange markets. For a small country that vitally depended on imports, the magnitude of the devaluation of the new national currency would be crucial. If the new currency were left entirely to the market, there would be a significant risk of a fall in its value that would go far beyond what would be warranted by restoring the competitiveness of the country's exports.

A deep devaluation, however, would cause constraints on the import side that would be hardly bearable. Oil and other commodities have to be imported and would become vastly more expensive after the depreciation. The prospect of having to call upon the IMF, shortly after the introduction of the new currency would be unacceptable. But this prospect could not be excluded as the vagaries of exit and the uncertainty about the future may drive demand for a country's currency significantly down in the short term. With international reserves of the central bank limited, the country would have few means to stem the tide against it.

To preclude such a poor outcome, cooperation with other countries would be the best option. If a number of smaller countries joined forces and exited together the effect of rising import prices could be mitigated to a certain extent (as fewer imports from outside the region would be needed – except for commodities like oil). Even more, pooling of reserves could be a way to increase the ability of all the exiting countries together to defend parities against international speculation.

A number of countries would also be in a better situation to nego- tiate a safety net to be provided by other EU countries or by the EU Commission. Countries considering exit from the EMU would obvi- ously think much harder before also exiting the EU at the same time. Continued membership of the EU could prove important in maintain- ing ties with the European common market, thus providing benefits from access to export markets once competitiveness would be restored. The EU has a moral and practical obligation to prepare for such a situ- ation, thus offering countries that are willing to take this big step a safe way out.

The EU could easily provide a safety net in the form of a monetary mechanism connected to EMU. It would be even possible to revive some of the mechanisms of the EMS that operated prior to the crea- tion of EMU, and which still exists formally. The new EMS could allow countries to peg their new currency at a reasonable rate to the Euro, thus reducing the risk of becoming a punching ball in the international financial markets. Such an 'orderly exit' of a group of countries would help preserve some of the achievements and the spirit of European partnership, without keeping countries in the straitjacket of EMU. The crisis has shown that the latter has tended sharply to exacerbate relations among European nations and to create a spirit of antagonism across Europe.

More broadly, it would be feasible for Europe to devise a system of managed exchange rates, even retaining a remnant of the Euro for some core countries, provided that the anchor country – Germany – agreed to deliver its role properly. It might even be feasible to devise a system of a common currency for the international transactions of the EU as a whole (or what would remain of it) i.e., a form of global means of payment and reserve holding, even while other member states still retained their national currencies. A structured arrangement of this type would allow for devaluations when necessary without resorting to cutting wages and imposing recessions. It would also allow for management of international trade and capital flows in Europe.

To this purpose it would be necessary to instigate permanent capital controls, to introduce public banking that could begin to reverse the failure of private banking in recent years, and to replace the ECB with an institution that could act as a fund managing the international transactions of Europe internally and externally. These changes would require democratisation of policy making, particularly in the sphere of finance. They would also require a restructuring of the enormous volumes of private and public debt that are currently burdening Europe.

Such changes would be impossible without abandoning neoliberalism as the framework for policy: austerity, liberalisation and deregulation have been the bane of policy making in Europe for decades. They would also be impossible without changing the existing, precise and carefully calibrated framework of treaties and institutions that have made the EU and the EMU what they are at present. Furthermore, Europe would need to change its tax policy in favour of taxing capital and the rich while moving towards profound income redistribution.

For both core and peripheral countries, the historic failure of the Euro is becoming an increasingly pressing issue. The longer the EMU persists in its current form, the stronger the risk of catastrophic collapse with unpredictable political repercussions. The sooner the Left across Europe realises what is at stake and offers realistic alternatives, the better for European societies as a whole.

CHAPTER 10

The Greek Catastrophe

The implications of the crisis and of the policies deployed by the troika as well as the awful predicament in which peripheral countries currently find themselves, are apparent in Greece, which has been affected more deeply than any other country in the Eurozone. The destructive impact on the economy is by now well understood and barely needs restating. Greece, however, also offers the prospect of an alternative strategy that could begin to heal the damage, while opening up a fresh path for other countries of the Eurozone periphery. For these reasons the Greek case is worth exploring in some detail in the remaining chapters of this book.

⊠. ECONOMIC AND SOCIAL COLLAPSE; WEAK GROWTH PROSPECTS

Some summary statistics would quickly establish the magnitude of the Greek disaster, thus facilitating analysis.[1] At the end of 2014, Greek GDP had contracted by more than 25 percent since the global crisis truly burst out in 2008, and by 22 percent since the introduction of the bailouts in 2010. Unemployment had exploded to 27.5 percent in 2013, representing 750,000 lost jobs since the intervention by the troika, two thirds of which were (in roughly equal proportions) in construction, manufacturing, and trade and retail. Industrial output had collapsed by roughly 35 percent since 2007, a decline that has occurred from an already low base reflecting the sustained de-industrialisation of Greece since the early 1980s. Wages, finally, declined by 27 percent in 2010–2014 contributing to a collapse of disposable incomes. The social impact of these developments has been simply devastating, with mass poverty

---

1   All figures are calculated by the authors from data provided by the Greek Statistical Authority at its portal, http://www.statistics.gr/portal/page/portal/ESYE.

emerging again in the country. There have even been phenomena approximating a humanitarian crisis in the urban centres.[2]

The application of austerity via the adjustment programmes of the troika, meanwhile, took the form of front-loaded reductions in public expenditure in 2010–12, followed by increases in taxation in 2013–14. The aim was to stabilise public finances and to generate primary budget surpluses – planned to reach an astonishing 4.5 percent of GDP in 2016 – with the aim of repaying the country's public debt. Indeed, government finances have swerved from an aggregate deficit of perhaps 15 percent of GDP in 2009 to a small primary surplus in 2014. The impact of this savage austerity on aggregate demand has been devastating, thus exacerbating the recession and unemployment. The impact on primary health provision, education, social security, and public transport, but also on the general capacity of the Greek state to deliver essential functions has been equally devastating.

However, if the purpose of the adjustment policies was to make Greek debt sustainable, the troika has failed altogether. After reaching a peak of 355bn euro in 2011, public debt was subjected to a bout of restructuring of privately owned debt (mostly held by domestic banks and various smallholders), which reduced its size to 304bn in 2012. Yet, debt rose again to more than 320bn by 2014. If debt is measured as proportion of GDP, moreover, the failure of policy is glaringly obvious: from 130 percent of GDP in 2009, when the fiscal crisis was about to erupt, debt reached 177 percent of GDP in 2014. The main reason for the rise of the debt ratio is, of course, the collapse of GDP induced by troika policies.

In this context, the prospects for recovery and growth in the foreseeable future are extremely poor, even though the gigantic recession that began in 2008 has gradually come to an end in 2014. The reasons are integral to the absurd adjustment policies imposed by the troika, and include the following:

i) The government cannot use fiscal policy to boost the economy since Greece is obliged by an array of bailout agreements, but also by the institutional mechanisms of the EU and the EMU, to maintain austerity by aiming at primary surpluses for the foreseeable future.

---

2   Journalists have been at the forefront of establishing this important point, see Geddes, 2012, and Politaki, 2013.

ii) Monetary policy is in the hands of the ECB, which has dramatically lowered interest rates in 2014. However, the beneficial effect for the economy is likely to be small since the banking system is weak and credit is contracting across Europe. Greek banks, in particular, are in an extremely precarious position given that up to 33 percent of their assets in 2014 were actually non-performing loans, the bulk of which were loans to enterprises. Not surprisingly, Greek banks have been deleveraging in recent years, and thus reducing the availability of liquidity and credit to the economy. Nonetheless, bank profits have been high since banks have been charging substantial spreads on lending.

iii) Consumption is very weak and likely to remain so given the collapse of wages, the rise in taxation and the large volumes of non-performing loans given for housing and general expenditure that are pressing down on households.

iv) Investment has been extremely weak since 2008 and is likely to remain so given the scarcity and high cost of bank credit. Taxation of SMEs has also increased significantly, thus impacting negatively on investment. Finally, there has been a collapse of trade credit accompanied by the spread of habits of non-payment among enterprises with the result that there has been a reversal of trade towards transacting for cash. The trend of transacting for cash is naturally very problematic for investment. There is, at last, neither reason nor evidence to back the expectation that there will be a wave of FDI to Greece sufficient to provide a major boost to the economy, leading it to sustained growth.

v) International trade is unlikely to prove a source of recovery, as even the EU is now acknowledging.[3] Imports have naturally collapsed, given the extraordinary depth of the recession, and exports picked up briefly in 2010–12. However, the rebound of exports appears to have been mostly due to Greek enterprises repositioning themselves as the domestic market collapsed. Much of the increase

---

3   Though its explanation in terms of missing 'institutional changes' is weak in both analytical and econometric terms, to put it mildly; see Böwer, Michou and Ungerer, 2014.

in exports during that period was actually to countries outside the EMU, a trend that is very much in line with the rest of the countries in the monetary union.[4] The weakness of the EMU economies since 2009, however, and the inability to devalue have proven a major impediment to Greek exports, which have faltered in 2013–14. The collapse of wages, after all, has not been enough sufficiently to boost competitiveness leading to strong growth of exports. Even worse, as the recession is coming to an end, imports have again been picking up strongly, with the result that the Greek trade account is showing signs of a widening deficit in 2014.

☒. THE PATH TO POVERTY AND HISTORICAL IRRELEVANCE

The picture that emerges for Greece in view of these trends is simply appalling. The country appears trapped in low-growth equilibrium with exceptionally high unemployment and without command over the instruments of economic policy that could alter its predicament. The notion that low wages coupled with deregulation of markets and privatisation of public assets would lead to sustained growth is entirely without theoretical and empirical foundation, as has been shown in detail throughout this book.

Moreover, Greece is weighed down by an enormous debt and bound by a series of agreements and institutional mechanisms set by the EU and the EMU forcing it to direct its economic activity towards servicing the debt. The only term that could adequately describe this state of affairs is debt peonage. Given the prospect of low growth and low incomes, Greece – already an ageing country – is likely to lose much of its trained youth to emigration, thus further weakening its long-term prospects. Income inequality is likely to increase and deep poverty to become a permanent feature of society. This is the price of the country remaining within the EMU and accepting the troika-imposed adjustment in 2010.

What will be the position of Greek capitalism in the world economy, if these eventualities come to pass? It is helpful in this context to be reminded that the crisis of 2007–9 was profound and structural, emanating from a deep transformation of mature capitalism in recent years

---

4   See O'Neill and Terzi, 2014, who find that EU countries, particularly those in the EMU, are trading less and less among themselves, while increasing their export reliance on other market.

that could be captured as the 'financialisation of capitalism'.[5] This is originally a Marxist term that describes a form of capitalism privileging financial transactions and encouraging the search for financial profit even among industrial and commercial enterprises. This type of capitalism is aggressively predatory and generates heavy household indebtedness wherever it takes root. It is also profoundly unequal and unstable, resulting in financial bubbles and crises periodically. Neoliberalism is the appropriate ideology of financialised capitalism, and it is no wonder that it has become so dominant in recent decades.

For a short while, during the crisis of 2007–9, it looked as if action might be taken to reverse financialisation, and to introduce different economic structures in mature countries, including the formation of public banks. But, since 2009, it has become clear that financialisation is deeply rooted and will not go away, not least because financial interests – above all, banks – wield enormous political power in developed and developing countries. The world will continue to move in the rut of financialisation for the foreseeable future.

Additional light could be cast on the creation of the EMU in Europe, if the monetary union was considered through the prism of financialisation, and bearing in mind the distinction between the domestic and the international roles of the Euro, which was discussed earlier in this book. Financialisation in Europe has been shaped by the common currency, the founding of which has been supported by big banks as well as by big businesses that are involved in financial transactions. Financialisation through the EMU in Europe has created a division between core and periphery, and the latter has so far borne the brunt of the crisis.

However, as the crisis has continued to simmer, even heavily financialised France has emerged as a historical loser, for reasons that were explained in previous chapters. Germany has become the dominant power of Europe, by drawing on tremendous wage restraint and consequent income tightness imposed on its own people. In this light, EU policies to deal with the crisis, adopted at the behest of Germany and supported by German exporting businesses and big banks, entail the continuation of the financialisation of Europe by sustaining the EMU in its current form.

In this emerging global and European order, Greece is heading for a subordinate position as a marginal and relatively poor country.

---

5   For further analysis of financialisation, see Lapavitsas, 2013.

The economy is likely to be dominated by a small number of relatively large enterprises that would be able to survive in international markets. Among these, banks are likely to remain the focus of attention of public policy, their interests protected at every turn. In contrast, SMEs will continue to face decimation, thereby profoundly changing the patterns of ownership of Greek capital. Unemployment, precarious employment and low incomes are likely to characterise the lives of the majority.

Meanwhile, public provision and welfare will continue to shrink, while the nation's patrimony will be gradually privatised at low prices, at the behest of the troika. The state will lose even more capabilities becoming increasingly dependent on the mechanisms of the EU and the EMU, as befits a debt peon. At the same time, it will continue to become increasingly authoritarian, governing by special decree when unpopular decisions have to be taken and relying on the security forces. Corruption and patronage will become thoroughly embedded in this structure, sustained by an alliance between big business and the state. This is the road to historical irrelevance for Greece, in the embrace of the deeply dysfunctional EMU.

CHAPTER 11

An Alternative Path for Greece

It is clear from the preceding analysis that, in the first instance, Greece requires urgent action to reverse the damage wrought by the inherent dysfunctionality of the monetary union, the recession and the adjustment policies of the troika. It is equally clear, however, that the required programme must simultaneously set the terms for a deep social transformation of the country in the interests of working people, shifting the balance away from big business and other forms of capital that have dominated and benefitted from the policy agenda for decades.

Note that the required alternative programme for Greece would have some applicability to other peripheral countries, but less so to the countries of the core. The extent of economic, social and political destruction in the periphery is far greater, as is the need for immediate action. More broadly, however, the position of core and peripheral countries within the EMU is quite different. Core countries are in pivot position to reconsider the failed project of the monetary union as a whole, potentially replacing it with a system of managing exchange rates as well as international transactions and debt, along the lines suggested in previous chapters of this book.

Analytically, then, the question of the alternative programme is considered in the rest of this book by focusing specifically on Greece and bearing in mind the predicament of other peripheral countries. In this light, there are six integrally connected issues that such a programme for Greece ought to confront in ways that would be in the interests of working people, thus acting as a template for the periphery.

⊠. National Debt: The Imperative of a Deep Write-Off

No alternative programme would be plausible in Greece without first settling the debt issue. This is not only because of the heavy annual cost currently imposed by the debt but also because the policy framework imposed by the troika is fundamentally shaped by the requirement of servicing the debt.

The sustainability of public debt is primarily a matter of flows, as was explained in detail in previous sections of this book. To be more specific, the flow of national income must be restored through growth to provide the wherewithal to service debt. The flow of fresh debt and of debt repayments must also be managed appropriately to prevent future debt crises. The appropriate policies to deliver these results clearly go beyond the topic of debt and also relate to the topics of growth and public finance, both of which are discussed below.

Debt sustainability, however, also refers to the stock of debt which has become unmanageable in several peripheral countries. Restructuring the stock of Greek debt will require write-offs, a policy that is inevitably confrontational since it would involve default, extended negotiations and usually considerable legal proceedings. It is of paramount importance, therefore, that the restructuring of debt should be handled with full transparency by a government of the Left. This means direct involvement by the citizenry, opening the books of the national debt to public scrutiny, and exercising democratic control over the entire process of restructuring. A useful step in this process would be the establishment of a Debt Audit Commission.

Since 2010, Greece has tried the solutions for its debt problem that were recommended by its creditors but to little noticeable effect. Securing resources to ensure the payment of debt has been the overriding concern of budgetary policy. The country has implemented harsh austerity measures and negotiated with its creditors an organised debt restructuring in 2011–12 that basically imposed a significant haircut on domestic holders, including banks. And yet, precisely because of the disastrous nature of troika policies, by 2014 the debt had reached 177 percent of GDP, or 4 percent higher than at the previous peak reached in 2012.[1] Even worse, as Figure 9 shows, under current policies determined by the bailout agreements, the future path of Greek debt is simply appalling.

Figure 9 demonstrates the projected evolution of Greek public debt based on IMF assumptions. Without a change in current policies, it will take twenty-six years of austerity for Greece to reduce its debt to levels consistent with the Maastricht Treaty. The assumptions made for this

---

1   See European Commission, 2014b.

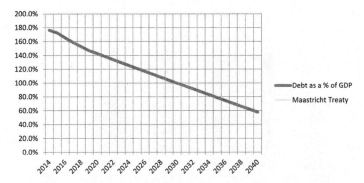

Fig. 9: The path of Greek debt under current policies – Debt as % of GDP
Sources: IMF World Economic Outlook 2014; Author projections

projection include an average annual interest rate of 3.6 percent (consistent with current levels and with the IMF projections), growth rate of 2.8 percent, and a primary surplus of 4.2 percent of GDP. Note that the growth rate projected is slightly above the historical average of the last fifty years. Furthermore, no country in history has been able to sustain primary surpluses for periods over ten years. In short, the conditions under which the country would reduce its debt to Maastricht levels by 2040 on the basis of IMF assumptions could only exist on an excel spreadsheet.

Despite its inability to control debt as proportion of GDP, the Greek government has continued to commit increasingly large volumes of resources to servicing a debt that realistically cannot – and should not – be repaid for economic, social and political reasons. Even after the debt restructuring in 2011–12, the government has devoted the staggering sum of 146.6bn Euros servicing debt in 2012 and 2013.[2] Taking only interest payments into account, for each Euro that the government has devoted to investment in 2012 and 2013, it has paid its creditors 1.43bn euros. A country that systematically devotes more resources to its creditors than to public investment and to the provision of public goods cannot be expected to grow, much less to overcome an economic crisis of historic proportions.

---

2   Debt service comprises amortisations and interest payments; see Ministry of Finance of Greece, 2014.

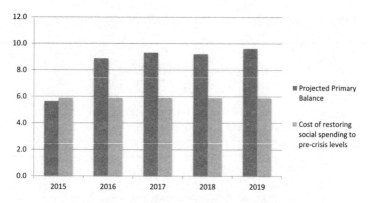

Fig. 10: The cost of debt-related austerity in Greece –
projected official primary balance (€ billions)

Sources: IMF World Economic Outlook 2014; Eurostat; Author projections

Furthermore, the welfare cost of continuing to impose austerity to service the debt in the future will be staggering. As Figure 10 shows, the country is expected to save roughly 40bn euros in the next five years to pay its creditors. But it would take only 30bn euros to restore expenditure on health, housing and education to pre-crisis levels. This is the quantitative side of debt peonage.

Specifically, Figure 10 shows the cost in billions of euros of the savings imposed on Greece by the Troika to fulfil the conditions of debt sustainability according to the bailout programmes. They are compared to the cost of restoring health, housing and education spending to pre-crisis levels.

It is sometimes suggested in current political debate that Greece should have a reduction on the interest rates of its loans. By any reasonable calculation, if that were accepted, it would probably mean no more than an additional reduction of gross debt by 5 percent of GDP by 2019.[3] Furthermore, it would require an additional twenty-six years of austerity to bring down public debt to a level consistent with the Maastricht Treaty. An alternative is required. Greece cannot and should not be forced to pay its public debt under current terms. The Greek people cannot be expected to submit to an endless process of decreasing

---

3   See Lapavitsas and Munevar, 2014.

living standards in the name of a goal that is economically impossible to achieve.

The alternative must start with a decisive reduction of the stock of debt, a deep write-off that could even amount to hundreds of billions of Euro. A write-off that would, for instance, be commensurate with the currently disastrous state of Greek society would be to reduce debt to Maastricht levels of 60 percent of GDP (a reduction of roughly 200bn euro). In that case, the government would have at least an additional 10bn euros annually to ensure the adequate provision of public goods and services required for the attainment of the economic, social and cultural rights of Greek citizens, while maintaining a prudent fiscal stance.[4]

A write-off would, of course, involve losses for the creditors to Greece. It is, therefore, necessary at this point to have a closer look at the composition of the public debt of Greece.[5] In 2009, as the Greek debt crisis was about to burst out, Greek public debt stood at 300bn euros (130 percent of GDP); it peaked in 2011 reaching 355bn euros (170 percent of GDP) before falling to 304bn euros (or 157 percent of GDP) in 2012. However, by the end of 2013 Greek public debt had again risen to about 320bn euros (174 percent of GDP).

The drop in public debt in 2012 was the result of restructuring, the so-called Private Sector Involvement (PSI), which affected roughly 200bn euros of privately held debt, imposing a deep write-off in the region of 50 percent of nominal value as well as a debt buy-back. The bulk of the losses fell on Greek holders, including banks, social security institutions and small bondholders. Losses to banks were made good through fresh public borrowing, thus limiting the final reduction of public debt.

Apart from the PSI default, Greek public debt has been thoroughly restructured during the years of the crisis in four important ways:

i) The composition of the debt has been altered dramatically since 2010, when debt comprised primarily bonds governed by Greek law. At the end of 2013 Greek public debt comprised mainly long-term loans provided by official lenders under the terms of the two bailout programmes in 2010 and 2011. To be more specific, out of 320bn euros of Greek debt at the end of 2013, roughly 65bn (20 percent)

---

4   Ibid.

5   Analysis below draws heavily on Lapavitsas and Munevar, 2014.

was still in the hands of private lenders, another 65bn (20 percent) was held by the ECB and the IMF, and the remaining 190bn (60 percent) had been advanced by the EU and the European Financial Stability Facility (EFSF). Thus, about 80 percent of Greek public debt is currently in the hands of official lenders and the governing law is typically non-Greek.

ii) The weighted average annual cost of Greek debt fell precipitously from just over 4 percent in 2009 to just over 2 percent in 2012, though it seems to have crept up above 3 percent in 2013.

iii) The weighted average maturity of Greek debt was extended significantly, rising from a little under eight years in 2009 to sixteen years in 2013.

iv) EU loans have provisions for extended grace periods, and therefore the maturity profile of government debt has improved substantially. During 2016–2036 Greece will face reduced annual repayments varying mostly between 5bn euros and 10bn euros.

Despite these profound changes in the volume and composition of debt, the Greek economy has been extremely weakened and can hardly cope with the current burden of public debt, as has already been shown. A deep write-off is called for and given the composition of the debt the bulk losses will fall on the public purse of EU countries, mostly those of the core. Needless to say, this would be a very difficult objective to achieve politically, and would require unilateral action by Greece, including declaring a temporary cessation of payments and implementing an integral public audit of the debt. Drawing on the results of this audit, but also mobilising the historical experience of several previous debt write-offs, it would be possible to reduce the stock of Greek debt to a level that would be compatible with the needs and rights of the Greek people. Europe must understand that public finance should be deployed to satisfy the needs of the people and not of big capital. Only by releasing Greece from the shackles of debt could the country return to growth and a dignified standard of living.

⊠. Lifting of Austerity: Neither Fiscal Surpluses, Nor Balanced Budgets

The current framework of Greek fiscal policy is determined, first, by the requirement of servicing the national debt and, second, by the strict rules of the EMU. Therefore, Greece has applied tremendous austerity by cutting expenditures and imposing tax increases on already reduced incomes. The short-term aim has been to achieve very large primary surpluses (up to 4.5 percent of GDP in 2016) to continue to repay the national debt. In the longer term, the country will have to follow a tight fiscal policy under the auspices of the EU, thus permanently avoiding deficits.

Figure 11 shows clearly the collapse of government expenditure after 2009 but also the decline in aggregate tax revenue, despite the tremendous increase in rates and forms of tax, as the economy went into severe recession.

The underlying reality of the tax storm imposed on the economy is apparent in Figure 12, which again shows the decline in aggregate tax revenue, while revenue from individual and household income *rises* and revenue from corporate profits *falls*. There is little doubt that is an economy that is basically killing itself.

The adoption of such gigantic austerity in the midst of a deep recession represents very bad economics indeed, and has been tremendously

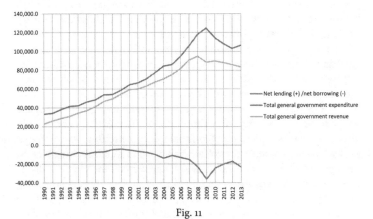

Fig. 11

Source: Eurostat; Author calculations

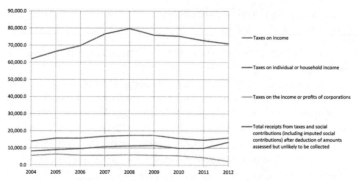

Fig. 12: Greek national accounts tax aggregates;
Breakdown of taxes on income, euro millions

Sources: Eurostat; Author calculations

destructive in terms of output, employment, the welfare state and the general capabilities of the state apparatus. A government of the Left should reject wholesale the policy of fiscal tightness, and even of balanced budgets. The main aim of fiscal policy ought to be the revitalisation of the economy, rather than servicing the debt, or complying with disastrous EU rules. In a depressed economy such as Greece, with 1.3 million unemployed and vast un- or underutilised resources, expansionary fiscal policy is absolutely necessary. Budget deficits for limited periods of time should be tolerated as they are likely to generate tax income once the economy picks up speed.

There would be two immediate sources of finance for an appropriate fiscal policy adopted by a government of the Left. First, a significant debt write-off and the attendant cessation of payments would provide substantial resources, as was shown above; second, there could be emergency public borrowing in the internal market with special purpose bonds. Writing off a large part of the national debt, in particular, would be a decisive step in adopting a fiscal policy aiming at generating employment, improving the living conditions of the people, strengthening the vital areas of health and education, and revitalising the economy. As was already mentioned above, a write-off compatible with Maastricht levels of national debt could provide Greece with an additional 10bn euros (5.4 percent of GDP) of fiscal space per year for the implementation of fiscal measures that could repair the damage done by austerity, while rebuilding public provision.

If, finally, a Left government also acquired monetary sovereignty, there could be monetisation of fiscal deficits for limited periods. There is no evidence that the issuing of money in extraordinary volumes as part of Quantitative Easing in Japan, the USA and the UK at various periods during the last two decades has boosted inflation significantly. The least of the worries of a government of the Left in Greece at the present moment should be inflation, particularly as the country is already in a state of deflation.

In a little more detail, on the expenditure side the focus of fiscal policy must be on helping the Greek people to get back to work, while also restoring the welfare state. An initial set of measures should revolve around the implementation of a Job Guarantee Programme to create publicly funded employment at the community level. A recent study has offered carefully derived estimates that such a programme could help create up to 550,000 new jobs at an estimated net cost of 4.2bn euros.[6] It has to be observed that the study is not particularly clear on the likely sources of funding for such programmes, which would naturally require a significantly higher initial outlay than the net expenditure of 4.2bn until tax revenues from expanded employment started to come in. It is highly unlikely, for instance, that European funds would be available for this purpose. If, however, there was a deep debt write-off, a Left government would have immediate access to funds that could be used to boost employment through such programmes. In this context, priority should clearly be given to community projects in tackling local unemployment.

A further set of expenditures should be aimed at rebuilding the Greek welfare state. The objective would be to increase the coverage and quality of the provision of public goods to regenerate trust in public institutions while also boosting the disposable income of households. Urgent and large-scale measures would include restoring primary health care and social support, providing relief to homeless families and individuals, whose numbers have increased in an unprecedented way for a European country during the crisis, providing food support to meet the wide and chronic demand, particularly in urban centres, and reconnecting the electricity network to those who have been cut off.

Once the immediate need of assuaging the destruction of social life by the austerity policies has been dealt with, fiscal policy would have to

6   See Antonopoulos, 2014.

turn to rebalancing of the economy in the direction of growth and social justice. A well-specified industrial policy would be vital in this regard. The main aim of fiscal policy as part of industrial policy would be to support a programme of public investment in infrastructure, research and development and education. Some further aspects of these policy aims are discussed below.

On the revenue side of fiscal policy, measures should be immediately taken to reduce the tax burden on households and SMEs with the aim of promoting employment and boosting disposable income.[7] Several options are available, which need careful costing to ensure neutrality in terms of revenue. These include:

i) An increase in the threshold of taxable income to boost the disposable income of households including those at, or near, the middle of the income distribution.

ii) A reduction of the VAT rates focusing particularly on items of popular consumption.

iii) Abolition of the recently approved general tax on real estate, to be replaced by a tax on households owning large real estate. Inheritance duties must also be raised for households that own large real estate.

iv) Rebalancing of Corporate Income Tax to favour SMEs and the creation of employment. A progressive tax scale should be designed to raise the burden on MNCs while lowering that on SMEs. Furthermore, the employer contributions by SMEs could be lowered and the revenue loss could be compensated by higher corporate taxes on MNCs. These measures would foster capital formation in the economy as a whole.

v) Raising the tax rate on dividends, interest and capital gains.

vi) Introducing a wealth tax.

---

7   In view of the destructive impact of heavy taxation on the Greek economy, a government of the Left would do well to be careful about proposals to raise taxes, particularly if it is imagined that tax increases could be a solution for the crisis. An economy as depressed as the Greek one needs a lessening, not an increase, of the tax burden.

To countermand the impact of tax-reducing policies on the revenue side, complementary strategies should be adopted aimed at tax evasion. Even four years into severe austerity and bailout policies, most of the burden of adjustment has been borne by easy-to-tax salaried employees and pensioners, while the rich have continued to stay out of the tax net, as even the IMF recognises.[8] It is imperative to alter this state of affairs, as it has been estimated that tax evasion by the well-off amounts to 7–9bn euros per year.[9] At the very least, there must be a strengthening and refinement of the penalties for large-scale tax evaders. The National Tax Agency should continue to be reformed and strengthened by increasing its personnel and improving its remuneration.

◻. THE BANKING SYSTEM: FAILURE OF PRIVATE BANKING AND THE NEED FOR NATIONALISATION

Private banking has failed in Greece and the costs to the country have been substantial. Prior to 2008 the balance sheets of private banks grew rapidly, from 181bn euros in December 1999 to 544bn euros in June 2010, however this lending was not directed to socially important activities and much of it was of poor quality.

First, only a small part of bank balance sheets was dedicated to lending to non-financial enterprises. The balance of such lending grew from 53bn euros in January 2001 (the earliest available data by the ECB) to 123bn euros in June 2010 – comprising just 23 percent of total assets at that point.[10]

Second, the crisis has revealed that the investments that fuelled the growth in total bank assets were of poor quality: private Greek bank capital needs were estimated at 50bn euros in December 2012.[11] As a result the banking system has been repeatedly bailed out using a combination of funds from the troika and the Greek state. The bailouts of banks were a key reason for the tremendous austerity imposed on the country. Specifically, Greek banks have received ample central bank liquidity without which they would have failed completely. At its peak, in July 2012, the Greek central bank had claims on domestic Monetary

---

8   See IMF, 2013.

9   See Artavanis, Morse, and Tsoutsoura, 2012.

10   Figures estimated by the authors from the ECB Statistical data warehouse.

11   See Bank of Greece, 2012.

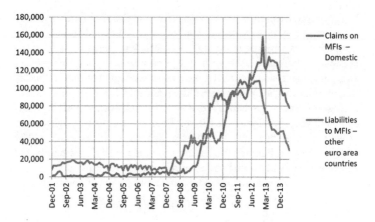

Fig. 13: Bank of Greece Balance Sheet – Liabilities to MFIs in other Euro area
countries & Claims on Domestic MFIs; euro millions

Source: Bank of Greece

Financial Institutions that were valued at 135bn euros as well as 13.2bn
euros of loans and securities to the domestic government.

Figure 13 shows the extent of liquidity support provided by the
Bank of Greece to domestic banks and to the government up to the
peak of the financial crisis in 2012. The Bank of Greece has obviously
relied on liquidity received from the ECB and the ESCB, as is apparent from the rapid increase of its liabilities during the same period.
The turning point at the end of 2012 came when Germany, through
its Chancellor Angela Merkel, essentially let it be kown that it would
not force Greece out of the Eurozone for the time being. After that, the
extent of support given to private banks but also the liquidity received
by the Greek Central Bank from the ECB and the ESCB has declined
precipitously.

Moreover, Greek private banks have received enormous capital
injections from both the Greek state and the troika. By the end of 2013
the Hellenic Financial Stability Fund (HFSF, the capital of which was
provided by the EFSF and increased to 49.7bn euros in 2013) held:
invested capital in the four systemic banks valued at 22.5bn euros, undis-
tributed EFSF securities for further capital injections valued at 10.3bn
euros, a derivative liability of 2.2bn euros and accumulated losses of
15.3bn euros. A good proportion of the losses arose from recapitalising

banks which were subsequently sold at a loss to the four systemic banks to whom the HFSF provided capital.[12]

Despite this assistance, in 2014 the state of the banks was far from healthy. Greek banks had one of the highest ratios of non-performing loans in the world at 31.3 percent of total gross loans at the end of 2013. Non-performing loans increased tremendously in the course of the recession, reaching perhaps 80bn euros in 2014, perhaps 45bn of which comprised business loans and the rest household loans (mortgages and consumer loans).[13]

Furthermore, banking is a business founded on the confidence that bank liabilities will be paid in full and on time. One barometer of this confidence is the volume of money that banks – the economy's arbiter of credit worthiness – lend to each other. Its size has been falling steadily since the onset of the crisis despite the efforts of the troika and the Greek state to rejuvenate the banks and the interbank market. Greek private banks owed to other domestic private banks 9bn euros in June 2010 but just 2.7bn in June 2014. Similarly, they owed to private banks of the other euro area 60.4bn euros in June 2010 but only 8.1bn Euros in June 2014.[14] In short Greek banks appeared to be carrying a huge proportion of non-performing loans, while being largely cut off from other European banks and lending very little to each other. These were unmistakable signs of a failing banking system.

The result has been that, after intensifying the economy's dependence on debt during the boom years in the 2000s, the banks have found themselves trapped in a spiral of deleveraging that has denied credit to the economy during the recession. Thus, fiscal austerity has been reinforced by a bank credit crunch. Figure 14 shows the rapid shrinkage of both assets and liabilities by Greek banks. Decline of bank lending together with a high interest rate on new loans has crippled economic activity.

In a little more detail, bank balance sheets have shrunk from 544bn euros in June 2010 to 397bn euros in July 2014, and lending to domestic non-financial enterprises has fallen from 124bn euros to 95bn euros in the same period. The trend is similar for bank lending to households: there was too much – badly judged – lending during the boom

---

12   Hellenic Financial Stability Fund, 2013.

13   Figures estimated from the ECB Statistical Warehouse. See also World Bank http://data.worldbank.org/indicator/FB.AST.NPER.ZS.

14   Figures estimated from the ECB Statistical Warehouse.

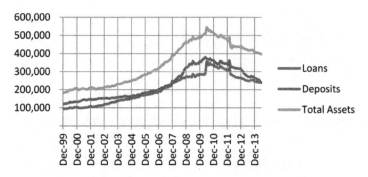

Fig.14: Greek MFIs (excl ESCB) aggregated balance sheets:
total assets, loans and deposits (euro millions)

Source: ECB

(from 31.9bn euros in January 2003 to 124bn euros in June 2010) while tight conditions have prevailed during the bust (lending falling to 112.7bn euros in June 2014).[15] The result was that households have been squeezed by the banks, and in turn have become ever worse credit risks and thereby increasing non-performing loans. To cap it all, the private banks have entered a spiral of deleveraging, their weakness has led to a restriction of credit, the economy has been further weakened, and this has led to further worsening of the position of the banks.

With few prospects of breaking out of this vicious cycle under current policies, and with still fewer structural changes undertaken by the EU to prevent the pattern from repeating itself, it is time for a change of direction. The banks ought to be properly nationalised and placed under public administration and democratic control. After a full public audit, bad debts would be removed and a healthy banking system would be created based on public capital. A national development bank would also be created to support long-term growth projects. Moreover, debt forgiveness for households ought to be introduced on the basis of public guarantees/capital for the lenders. The nationalised banking system would engage in expansion of short-term credit and liquidity provision, particularly to SMEs that comprise the backbone of the Greek economy. The purpose would be to revitalise economic activity in the short-term and to boost employment.

---

15   The figures have been estimated from the ECB Statistical Warehouse.

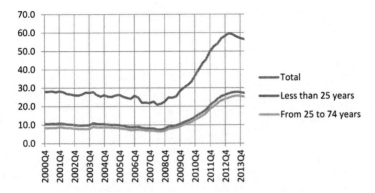

Fig. 15: Unemployment rate by age group (quarterly average, %)

Source: Eurostat

⊠. RELIEVING THE WORST OF THE CRISIS AND RESTORING LABOUR MARKET CONDITIONS

Unemployment has ravaged wage earners in Greece and the collapse in incomes has negatively affected those still in employment. Figure 15 shows the explosive increase in unemployment in the course of the crisis, which has reached extraordinary levels for young people.

The OECD notes that 'the largest impacts of the crisis on people's well-being have come through lower employment and deteriorating labour market conditions [and] the poor employment situation had a major impact on life satisfaction'.[16] The loss of employment, the fall in wages, and the decline in public provision have created dramatic conditions for much of the population with regard to basic goods, such as food, energy, medicines and housing. Official statistics struggle to capture the misery in which a large swathe of the population finds itself.

However, Figures 16 and 17 show, respectively, the extraordinarily rapid increase in severe material deprivation and the collapse in health expenditure per capita since the adoption of the bailouts. The sudden emergence of these trends has pushed Greece violently in the direction of developing countries.

Further sources of information paint an even worse picture:

---

16   See OECD, 2014.

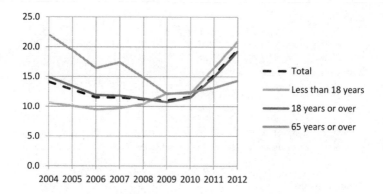

Fig. 16: Severe material deprivation (% of total population)
Source: Eurostat

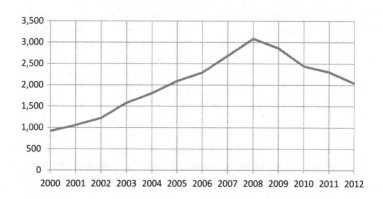

Fig. 17: Health expenditure per capita (current US$)
Source: World Bank

i) Homelessness has risen markedly: the Red Cross quotes a 20–25 percent increase in the numbers of people living on the streets, and the organisation has expanded its social programmes to try and cope with the emerging humanitarian crisis.[17] In addition those that are not actually on the streets are often living in crowded conditions. Young people in particular, with very little chance of employment and falling benefits, are staying at home, often surviving on the falling pensions and incomes of their parents.

ii) Turning to health, there appears to be a chronic drug shortage, while official statistics show that health expenditure per capita, rising throughout the 2000s, has fallen from US$3,000 to US$2,000 since 2008.[18] Deep cuts in public health care provision have resulted in long waiting times and reduced accessibility amid clear signs that 'health outcomes have worsened' already in 2011.[19]

iii) Perhaps even more alarming is that significant sections of the population are suffering from food poverty, with increasing numbers relying on food banks and around half of poor households with children finding themselves unable to supply a healthy diet, according to UNICEF.[20]

iv) Finally, fuel poverty has drastically increased, in regard to both heating homes and using private cars. Air quality in Athens and other large urban centres has declined dramatically in winter as residents have taken to burning wood, rubbish and other materials for warmth.

A Left government would have to confront the immediate reality of such poverty as well as dealing with its underlying causes. The economic recovery of the country must translate into immediate practical measures aimed at restoring the quality of life in Greece, if it is to gain popular support. The state should take the initiative, together with

---

17   See International Federation of Red Cross and Red Crescent Societies, 2013.

18   Estimated from data at http://data.worldbank.org/country/greece.

19   See Kentikelenis, et al., 2011.

20   See UNICEF, 2014.

community and associational organisations and international NGOs, such as the Red Cross, to cover the essential needs of Greek citizens, including shelter, food, medicine and energy at a basic level.

At the very least, households that have been cut off from the electricity networks should be reconnected, food provision to those facing severe food poverty should be nationally coordinated, and homelessness should be assuaged through the creation of shelters. On health care, the focus must be to reverse the negative trends of increasing child mortality and decreasing life expectancy that have occurred with the implementation of austerity. To this purpose, insured coverage must be increased to protect vulnerable households, eventually aiming at providing universal coverage. Expenditure must also be increased to provide primary health care with the added benefit that it would lower the expense of long-term medical care.

The fiscal cost of such policies would be modest, but it would still be necessary to abandon austerity, if they are to be implemented. The economic and political benefits, moreover, would be substantial. On the one hand, a boost to welfare would increase the disposable income of households, thus strengthening the recovery. On the other, stronger provision of public services and a supportive role for the state would be vital steps towards restoring the trust and confidence of the Greek people. Confronting tax evasion and immediately improving provision of public goods must go hand in hand.

More broadly, however, a Left government should tackle the causes of poverty and this implies three vital forms of action. First, reducing unemployment, as was discussed in Chapter 2.2. Second, raising wages and immediately restoring collective bargaining in the labour market by annulling the anti-labour laws passed since the bailout. Minimum wages should be restored from the current 586 euro per month to the original 751 euro. The impact on private enterprises, particularly SMEs, must be partly offset through tax relief, but also through the boost in demand that will result from the abandonment of austerity. Wages in general should be set in line with productivity growth and considerations of income redistribution in the future. Third, rebalancing the pension system to support the lowest pension holders, and thus to confront pensioner poverty. It ought to be stressed, however, that there could not be a long-term solution for the generally parlous state of the pension schemes in Greece without boosting employment. The ultimate answer to pension poverty is to lift austerity and boost growth.

⊠. Medium-Term Restructuring of the Productive Sector

A Left government would have to abandon the current neoliberal development strategy imposed by the troika which essentially comprises lowering wages, liberalising, privatising and hoping for spontaneous increase of domestic investment and FDI to generate growth. Greece needs a medium-term development strategy that would be based on industrial policy to boost growth rates, reduce unemployment and raise incomes, in an ecologically sustainable way. Formulating such a strategy and bringing it to bear would require the collective effort of social organisations, parts of the state apparatus, academics and organisations of civil society across the country. The most that could be done at this point is to spell out some of the fundamental issues involved.

The required industrial policy must first take into account the protracted deindustrialisation of the country, which started in the early 1980s and has become dramatic following the massive destruction of industrial capacity since 2007. It must also take into account the problematic nature of EU and EMU institutions and policies, which have led Greece to the current development impasse. Finally, it must be fully aware of the domination of key parts of the world market by large MNEs, which control technology and command supply chains.

It would be a fallacy, however, to think that under conditions of global financialised capitalism it is impossible to implement a development strategy for a medium-sized economy, such as Greece. The experience of the last three decades across the developing world shows that it is perfectly possible to devise an effective strategy for development and growth provided that the state and the private sector strike an appropriate balance. More specifically, Greece would need to boost its industry by paying attention to domestic demand as well as by changing the composition of output in favour of tradable goods. Such a strategy would inevitably depend on strengthening the SMEs that are still the backbone of the Greek economy, at the expense of large capital. It is also imperative for Greece to strengthen its agricultural sector which has steadily declined during the years of EU membership.

In the long term, the required development strategy for Greece would require a thorough revamp of the education system. In the shorter term, however, the strategy would rely on a coherent programme of public investment as well as a programme of public support for R&D. Fundamental to putting such a strategy in place would be the nationalisation of the banking system as well as the creation of publicly owned development banks. The development banks could be originally instituted as deposit-taking institutions but eventually, and as their loan portfolios would expand, they could issue bonds to provide a stable and sustainable basis for lending. Priority on loans should be given to SMEs in the tradable sectors, particularly those that would have the potential to insert themselves in international chains of value added.

☒. DEMOCRATISATION AND STATE TRANSFORMATION

The current state apparatus and the political parties and personnel that have run Greece for several decades are absolutely incapable of delivering these necessary changes. A Left government that sought to transform the country by relying on existing institutions would fail, and probably rapidly. Greece needs root and branch reform of both its state and polity in a democratic direction, if it is to enter on a different path of development.

In particular, the Greek state has been critically weakened during the last three decades losing a range of capabilities as a result of relying increasingly on EU mechanisms. Corruption has grown, shaped by big business interests, and frequently related to public procurement for the bloated military sector. The mechanisms of state have become increasingly authoritarian and the security forces appear to have become permeated by extreme right-wing networks. The state machinery has to be cleansed and democratised while also improving its capabilities in designing and delivering economic and social policy.

A vital part of this process would be re-establishing capacity in the economic arms of the state, above all, for the central bank and the economics ministries. Equally important would be re-establishing technical know-how on the Greek economy by reviving a host of publicly supported research institutes that have withered away during the last three decades. Even more important would be revamping the system of justice to deal with institutional delays, corruption and inability to enforce laws in a variety of areas, including that of honouring commercial and other debts.

Political reform would be paramount to effect these changes since the political system has thoroughly failed the country prior to and during the crisis. Greece needs new and participatory political mechanisms that are accountable and incorruptible. It also needs a new political dispensation that would include changes in the institutions of political representation, changes in its constitution and, at long last, a proper separation of church and state. Finally, the pockets of extreme right-wing authoritarianism, and even fascism, in the security forces will have to be confronted directly.

CHAPTER 12

A Ray of Hope for Greece and Europe

The Greek crisis has had such a devastating impact on the economy and society that Greek politics has been turned upside down. It is likely that a Left government, led by the current official opposition party, SYRIZA, would be formed in the near future, even in 2015. This would be a momentous event for Greece, and it might prove a turning point for Europe.

The officially announced programme of SYRIZA rests on two pillars. First, the party aims to achieve a substantial write-off of Greek public debt, albeit on a consensual basis. Second, it promises to lift austerity by aiming for balanced budgets, instead of the surpluses demanded by the current adjustment programme. The loosening of fiscal policy will allow for a series of measures to assuage the worst impact of the crisis, such as reconnecting families to the electricity network, providing food relief, and sheltering the homeless. It will also allow for immediate action to reduce unemployment through public programmes of the type discussed in the previous chapter. SYRIZA is also committed to raising the minimum wage, lowering the enormous tax burden and boosting public investment in an effort to accelerate growth.

There is nothing radical, much less revolutionary, to these policies. They represent the least that could and should be done to improve the dreadful state of Greece and to open a fresh path for other European countries. Note that SYRIZA has repeatedly declared its intention to keep the country within the EMU and to avoid unilateral actions on the issue of the public debt. There is little doubt that its leadership are committed Europeanists who truly believe that they could help transform the EU from within.

The trouble is, of course, that the EU and the EMU would be far from amenable to SYRIZA ideas. As was explained in earlier chapters of this book, Germany's exporters and banks have benefitted substantially from the euro, and have no incentive to abandon austerity.

Furthermore, in 2015 and beyond, Berlin is likely to be preoccupied with the persistent malfunctioning of the Eurozone as a whole, especially the troubled economies of France and Italy. The last thing that Germany would welcome would be SYRIZA and its programme.

SYRIZA appears to have the impression that it could achieve a deep debt write-off and a reversal of the policies of austerity while still remaining within the EMU, provided that it negotiated 'hard'. In other words, it hopes to attain precisely the 'impossible triad'. Its ostensible aim on the issue of Greek debt is to have a grand European conference that would confront debt across Europe, offering relief to peripheral countries, along the lines of the London Conference of 1953 that dealt with German public debt on favourable terms. Its hope is that Greece would be offered debt forgiveness on a substantial scale, a grace period for interest payments, and perhaps a replacement of much of the remaining debt with GDP-indexed bonds (so-called 'bisque' bonds) the repayment of which would be tied to growth rates.

There seems little realistic prospect of achieving such a settlement of debt on a consensual basis. The most likely form of debt relief that might be offered by the EU would be to lower interest rates and to extend the maturity of debt, including perhaps a period of grace on debt servicing. It is also conceivable that a small write-off of the principal might be granted as a gesture of goodwill. Such measures, however, would be unlikely to have a significant impact on the economy. Greece needs a deep debt write-off that would probably run in the hundreds of billions of euros. To be sure, a period of grace on debt servicing and easier terms of repayment, perhaps including a growth and employment clause, would be welcome, but they would hardly alter the basic macroeconomic outlook.

Moreover, in the absence of a political miracle, the EU would be extremely unlikely to offer debt relief that would be accompanied by a relaxation of conditionality, including lifting austerity, relaxing pressure on wages, and abandoning privatisations and deregulation. On the contrary, the EU would probably insist on continuing with the policies of fiscal rigidity and avoiding deficits, which are now formally embedded in its structure and entail monitoring and fines for 'delinquent' countries. Indeed, any EU concessions on Greek debt are likely to be accompanied by additional compensatory terms on fiscal policy, deregulation and privatisation. Otherwise it would be very difficult for the politicians of core countries to persuade their electorates of the need for Greek debt relief, while also keeping Greece in the EMU. Thus, even if a Left government was offered some dispensation on debt within the confines of the EMU, it would certainly not obtain the consent of the EU to change its fiscal policies drastically.

The 'impossible triad' cannot be evaded by a Left government in Greece, even if it had the most Europeanist intentions and truly modest policy aims. Indeed, a Left government in Greece can expect unrelenting hostility from the EU, which is not short of weapons. The SYRIZA programme might be modest, but it still lacks secure funding. SYRIZA intends to obtain at least half of the funds that would allow it to loosen fiscal policy by reducing tax evasion and collecting tax debts. This is optimistic and hopeful, to put it mildly. Greece also needs substantial finance to service its debts in 2015, as was already discussed in the previous chapter. And, needless to say, Greek banking would be rapidly asphyxiated if the ECB stopped providing liquidity. A Left government is likely to face an ultimatum to capitulate, perhaps by accepting some watered-down version of austerity. The threat of being forced out of the EMU is likely to be raised.

It is possible, of course, to imagine that the cost of conflict and potential exit of a peripheral country from the EMU would prove too great for the EU because it would have severe economic and political implications for the monetary union. On this basis, one could further imagine that a Left government would have a strong bargaining chip in its hands, and it could thus force the EU to accept debt write-offs and abandonment of austerity, while the country continued to remain in the EMU. There are forces within the Left in Greece, including in SYRIZA, which are close to this view. That might be, perhaps, what lies behind the rather incoherent claim that SYRIZA will negotiate 'hard'.

Unfortunately, this would be confused and dangerous thinking. The EU has shown clearly in the case of Cyprus in 2013 that it is prepared to contemplate exit – indeed, it was ready to force Cyprus out of the EMU. There is also plenty of evidence that the EU has seriously considered forcing Greece to exit during 2010–12. It would be foolish for a Left government to imagine that the EU would bluff on the issues of debt and austerity. The economic cost and the disruption caused by the exit of a peripheral country would indeed be substantial for the EU, but it would pale into insignificance compared to the cost of accepting debt write-offs and abandonment of austerity, while keeping Greece within the EMU. The current political and economic hierarchy of the EU is not about to commit suicide, and hence it would be implacably opposed to a radical programme by a small peripheral country. If a Left government attempted to play a bluffing game, it would fail very rapidly.

A SYRIZA government is likely to be disabused of its illusions rather rapidly. If it attempted to implement its programme, it would face major confrontation and conflict with the EU, that would also raise the prospect of exiting the monetary union. The outcome of such conflict cannot be predicted with certainty, and that is precisely where hope lies for both Greece and Europe. The hostility of the EU establishment and the existence of a dysfunctional and failing monetary union should not be accepted as binding constraints by a government of the Left that has the interests of working people foremost in its mind. SYRIZA should be prepared for conflict by mobilising its domestic strength, while also relying on considerable international support. The prospect of exiting the EMU is neither forbidding nor unmanageable, as has been shown earlier. More broadly, there is a profound and urgent need for change across Europe to free it from the absurd shackles of the euro. Those who make the first decisive steps in that direction would be able to rescue their own societies from decline as well as helping to put Europe down a different path of economic and social development.

Afterword: An Opportunity for Europe

Alberto Garzón Espinosa,
Izquierda Unida in Spain

For a long time, Europe was a synonym of progress for countries in southern Europe such as Spain, Portugal or Greece. They had all been under ruthless regimes and looked to northern Europe with hope. Values such as democracy, modernisation, social and civil rights were all said to be possible if the South joined the North in order to build a greater European Union.

The situation is different today, and the countries of the South are suffering the consequences of the crisis and of the neoliberal measures implemented during it. Austerity measures and national debt are the mechanisms which have been used in order to destroy the social achievements that the working class had obtained after years of struggle. National constitutions in these countries are being emptied of their content and positive guarantees, such as the right to employment or the right to housing, have been suspended. A large process of regression is taking place in all of Europe, and it is hitting the South most intensively.

But it is not the only crisis; we are dealing with a constituent process which started a long time ago. The current European Union and its architecture have been designed by a handful of bureaucrats who sought by all means to avoid any possible alternatives to neoliberalism. It is a project based on the liberal political tradition, with the fear of the people and of the full exercise of popular sovereignty at its base, and it has made the construction of the neoliberal project of civilisation possible. It is not only about the economy, it is a whole lifestyle.

However, we cannot only see neoliberalism as a strictly ideological phenomenon. It is not possible to contest neoliberal hegemony in the sphere of ideas alone. We are, in fact, witnessing a reorganisation of social classes both within the national economies and the global political economy. The neoliberal project aims to be a counterrevolution intending to abolish the social and economic achievements obtained during the post-war years. Thus, the neoliberal project is using the current European institutional framework, the European Union, as well as adapting national institutions, in order to obtain its goals. There are good examples of these structural reforms and other important changes in institutions, such as the constitutional reforms which were forced on countries.

The truth is that the current crisis has shown us the true face of the neoliberal project. The current European Union is not a supportive articulation of national economies or a project based on social construction, but a board game designed by big European capital in order to improve its position in the global economy. Financial capital in particular has been the main actor in the construction of the European Union and its successful goal has been to create a straightjacket to avoid all progressive policies. 'There is no alternative to neoliberalism' is the political guide for financial capital.

In this context, and with an absolutely exhausted accumulation regime in the southern countries, European institutions and neoliberal governments have accelerated the economic policies aimed at dismantling and destroying public services and social rights. They are therefore consolidating a radically regressive social model characterized by the lack of job stability and the rise of inequality. This will mean a radical reorganisation of social classes which will transform the social structures of the different countries completely.

Obviously, the troika's main goal is not the impoverishment of the population per se but to reshape the areas of profitability. But these new areas are only possible if a number of adjustment programmes are implemented by the governments. The adjustment programmes are pushing peripheral economies into a scenario of new economic growth and a new social model. The destruction of social conquests is a necessary requirement in order to achieve the neoliberal project because these rights are, today more than ever before, obstacles to capital gains. However, this path has taken the South into a new economic depression which is already underway, with high levels of unemployment, growing social exclusion, and other typical features of capitalism's crises, to which we have to add the new social order based on repression and authoritarianism which we are witnessing.

The description above is of their project, the one of the financial elites. But there is hope, and we have an alternative project. Today the spirit of political hope is abroad in Europe. We know that there is not a way out for the working class within the current European Union. A different political and economic integration is not only possible, but necessary – a republican and socialist integration, an integration preserving social conquests and human rights, and an integration which begins with the democratisation of the economy. We are aware that to get there we need a lot of audacity, pedagogy and solidarity, but we are also aware that we are not facing technical problems, but problems related to political will. Joan Robinson once said that 'the purpose of studying economics is not to acquire a set of ready-made answers to economic questions, but to learn how to avoid being deceived by economists'. Today there is a large army of bad economists recommending bad policies for the interest of a small minority. It has probably never been more important to offer different approaches.

Bibliography

Antonopoulos, R., 2014, 'Responding to the Unemployment Challenge: A Job Guarantee Proposal for Greece', April, Levy Economics Institute, Annandale on Hudson, New York, retrieved from http://www.levyinstitute.org/pubs/rpr_apr_14.pdf.

Artavanis, N., Morse, A. and Tsoutsoura, M., 2012, *Tax Evasion across Industries: Soft Credit Evidence from Greece*, retrieved from http://www.chicagobooth.edu/blogs/informingreform/docs/taxevasion.pdf.

Baldwin, R.E. and Wyplosz, C., 2004, *The Economics of European Integration*, Berkshire and London: McGraw-Hill Education.

Bank of Greece, 2012, 'Report on the Recapitalisation and Restructuring of the Greek Banking System', Athens, retrieved from http://www.bankofgreece.gr/BogEkdoseis/Report_on_the_recapitalisation_and_restructuring.pdf.

Bayer, N., 2002, *Wurzeln der Europäischen Union: Visionäre Realpolitik bei Gründung der Montanunion*, St. Ingbert, Röhrig Universitätsverlag.

Berens, A., 2002, *Der Weg der Europäischen Wirtschaftsgemeinschaft zur Politik des leeren Stuhls und zum Luxemburger Kompromiss* unpublished dissertation, University of Düsseldorf.

Blanchard, O. and Wyplosz, C., 2004, *Deux thèses hétérodoxes sur l'économie Européenne.* En Temps Réel, Cahier 14/15, Juin, retrieved from, http://entempsreel.com/deux-theses-heterodoxes-sur-leconomie-Europeenne.

Blanchard, O., 2007, 'Adjustment within the Euro: The Difficult Case of Portugal', *Portuguese Economic Journal*, 6 (1): 1–21.

Böwer, U., Michou, V. and Ungerer, C., 2014, 'The Puzzle of the Missing Greek Exports', 2014, European Commission, Economic Papers 518, retrieved from http://ec.Europa.eu/economy_finance/publications/economic_paper/2014/pdf/ecp518_en.pdf.

Brasche, U., 2003, *Europäische Integration: Wirtschaft, Erweiterung und regionale Effekt*, Munich: Ouldenbourg.

Davidson, P., 2013, 'Unsicherheit und staatliche Sparpolitik', in *Handelt jetzt! Das globale Manifest zur Rettung der Wirtschaft*, Frankfurt am Main: Westend Verlag.

Dechamps, E., 2007a, *The Council of Europe*, European Navigator, retrieved from http://www.ena.lu.

Dechamps, E., 2007b, *The Costums Union Projects*, European Navigator, retrieved from http://www.ena.lu.

Deutsche Bundesbank, 2007, *Monthly Report*, April, retrieved from http://www.bundesbank.de/volkswirtschaft/vo_monatsbericht_2007.php.

Deutsche Bundesbank, 1997, *Europäische Organisationen und Gremien im Bereich von Währung und Wirtschaft*, Frankfurt am Main: Deutsche Bundesbank.

European Central Bank, *Monthly Report January 2013*, Frankfurt am Main.

European Commision, 2013a, 'Commission Staff Working Document: Refining the MIR Scoreboard', Brussels, retrieved from http://ec.europa.eu/europe2020/pdf/2014/mipsb2014_swd_en.pdf.

European Commision, 2013b, 'European Economy: Macroeconomic Imbalances, France 2013', Occasional Papers 136, Brussels, retrieved from http://ec.europa.eu/economy_finance/publications/occasional_paper/2013/pdf/ocp136_en.pdf.

European Commision, 2014a, 'European Economy: Macroeconomic Imbalances, Germany 2014', Occasional Papers 174, Brussels, retrieved from http://ec.europa.eu/economy_finance/publications/occasional_paper/2014/pdf/ocp174_en.pdf.

European Commission, 2014b, 'Greece: Recovery Signs Strengthening', Brussels, retrieved from http://ec.Europa.eu/economy_finance/eu/forecasts/2014_spring/el_en.pdf.

European Union, 2007, *The History of the European Union*, retrieved from http://Europa.eu/abc/history/index_en.htm.

Flassbeck, H., 1988, *Preise, Zins und Wechselkurs – Zur Theorie der offenen Volkswirtschaft bei flexiblen Wechselkursen*, Wirtschaftswissenschaftliche und wirtschaftsrechtliche Untersuchungen des Walter Eucken Instituts (23), Tübingen, J.C.B. Mohr (Paul Siebeck).

Flassbeck, H., 1997, *Und die Spielregeln für die Lohnpolitik in einer Währungsunion? Frankfurter Rundschau*: 12.

Flassbeck, H. and Lapavitsas, C., 2013, 'The Systemic Crisis of the Euro: True Causes and Effective Therapies', Rosa Luxemburg Stiftung Studien, retrieved from http://www.Rosalux.de/fileadmin/rls_uploads/pdfs/Studien/Studien_The_systemic_crisis_web.pdf.

Flassbeck, H. and Spiecker, F., 2000, *Löhne und Arbeitslosigkeit im internationalen Vergleich*, Study for the Hans-Böckler-Stiftung und den Bundesvorstand des DGB, retrieved from http://www.flassbeck.de/pdf/2000/LoehneundArbeit.pdf.

Flassbeck, H. and Spiecker, F., 2005, 'Die deutsche Lohnpolitik sprengt die Europäische Währungsunion', *WSI-Mitteilungen*, 58 (12): 707–713.

Flassbeck, H., Davidson, P., Galbraith, J.K., Koo, R. and Ghosh, J., 2013, *Handelt jetzt! Das globale Manifest zur Rettung der Wirtschaft*, Frankfurt am Main: Westend Verlag.

Geddes, L., 2012, 'Greece in Crisis: Saving a Nation,' *New Scientist*, 214 (2866) 26 May: 6–8.

Gros, D. and Thygesen, N., 1998, *European Monetary Integration*, 2nd edition, Harlow and Essex: Longman.

Harbrecht, W., 1984, *Die Europäische Gemeinschaft*, 2nd edition, Stuttgart: UTB für Wissenschaft.

Hellenic Financial Stability Fund, *Annual Report 2013*, retrieved from http://www.hfsf.gr/files/hfsf_annual_report_2013_en.pdf.

Holtfrerich, 2007, *Post-1945 Western European Integration: The Foster Child of Vision, Crisis and Persistent Search for Compromise*. Mimeo.

IMF, 1995, *World Economic Outlook*, Washington, DC: International Monetary Fund.

IMF, 2013, 'Greece. Selected Issues: IMF Country Report No. 13/155', retrieved from http://www.imf.org/external/pubs/ft/scr/2013/cr13155.pdf.

International Federation of Red Cross and Red Crescent Societies, 2013, 'The "Quiet Desperation" of Homeless People in Greece', retrieved from https://www.ifrc.org/en/news-and-media/news-stories/Europe-central-asia/greece/the-quiet-desperation-of-homeless-people-in-greece-60635/.

Issing, O., et al., 2006, 'Are German Workers Killing Europe?', *International Economy*, 20 (3): 37–45.

Kalecki, M., 1944, 'Three Ways to Full Employment', in *Collected Works of Michal Kalecki, Volume I*, Oxford: Oxford University Press.

Kentikelenis, A., Karanikolos M., Papanicolas I., Basu S., McKee M. and

Stuckler D., 2011, 'Health Effects of a Financial Crisis: Omens of a Greek Tragedy', *Lancet* 387 (9801): 1457–1458.

Keynes, J.M., 1929, 'The German Transfer Problem'. *Economic Journal*, 39: 1–7.

Keynes, J.M., 1930, 'A Treatise on Money – The Pure Theory of Money', in *The Collected Writings of John Maynard Keynes, Volume V*, London and Basingstoke: Macmillan 1973.

Keynes, J.M., 1936, 'The General Theory of Employment, Interest and Money', in *The Collected Writings of John Maynard Keynes, Volume VII*, London and Basingstoke: Macmillan 1973.

Koo, R., 2008, *The Holy Grail of Macroeconomics: Lessons from Japan's Great Recession*, Singapore: Wiley.

Krugman, P., 1991, 'Has the Adjustment Process Worked?', *Policy Analyses in International Economics* 34, Institute for International Economics.

Krugman, P., 1992, 'Exchange Rates and the Balance of Payments', in *Currency and Crises*, Cambridge, MA: MIT Press.

Krugman, P., 1998, 'What happened to Asia?'. presentation at a conference in Japan, retrieved from http://web.mit.edu/krugman/www/DISINTER.html.

Krugman, P., 2013a, 'Fallacies of Immaculate Causation', *New York Times*, 16 October, retrieved from http://krugman.blogs.nytimes.com/2013/10/16/fallacies-of-immaculate-causation/?_r=2.

Krugman, P., 2013b, 'More Notes on Germany', *New York Times*, 1 November, retrieved from http://krugman.blogs.nytimes.com/2013/11/01/more-notes-on-germany/

Lapavitsas, C. 2013, *Profiting without Producing: How Finance Exploits Us All*, London and New York: Verso.

Lapavitsas, C., et al., 2012, *Crisis in the Eurozone*, London and New York: Verso.

Lapavitsas, C., and Munevar, D., 2014, 'Greece Needs a Deep Debt Write Off', Occasional Policy Paper #10, *Research on Money and Finance*, retrieved from http://www.researchonmoneyandfinance.org/images/occasional_policy_papers/RMF-OPP-10-Lapavitsas-Munevar.pdf

McKinnon, R., 2012, *The Unloved Dollar Standard: From Bretton Woods to the Rise of China*, Oxford: Oxford University Press.

Merkel, A., 2013, speech at the World Economic Forum in Davos, retrieved from http://www.bundeskanzlerin.de/Content/EN/

Reden/2013/2013-01-24-merkel-davos.html.

Melitz, J., 1987, *Monetary Discipline, Germany, and the European Monetary System*, IMF Working Paper No. 87/6.

Milward, A.S., 2003, *The Reconstruction of Western Europe, 1945–51*, Berkley: University of California Press.

Milward, A.S. and Sorensen, V., 1993, 'Interdependence or Integration? A National Choice', in Milward, A.S., et al., eds, *The Frontier of National Sovereignty: History and Theory 1945–1992*, London and New York: Routledge.

Milward, A.S., 2002, *The Rise and Fall of a National Strategy 1945–1963*, London: Frank Cass Publishers.

Ministry of Finance of Greece, 2014, 'State Budget Execution Monthly Bulletin, December 2013', Athens, retrieved from http://www.minfin.gr/content-api/f/binaryChannel/minfin/datastore/c8/c2/4e/c8c24ef3e8c5b5690cb8bc61c944cfced5145b0a/application/pdf/Bulletin_12_2013.pdf.

Monnet, J., 1978, *Erinnerungen eines Europäers*, Munich: Deutscher Taschenbuch-Verlag.

Neuss, B., 2000, *Geburtshelfer Europas? Die Rolle der Vereinigten Staaten im Europäischen Integrationsprozess 1945–1958*, Baden-Baden: Nomos Verlag.

O'Neill, J. and Terzi, A., 2014, 'Changing Trade Patterns, Unchanging European and Global Governance', Bruegel Working Paper 2014/02, retrieved from http://www.bruegel.org/publications/publication-detail/publication/817-changing-trade-patterns-unchanging-European-and-global-governance/.

Obstfeld, M. and Rogoff, K., 1996, *Foundations of International Macroeconomics*, Cambridge, MA: MIT Press.

OECD, 1994, *The OECD Jobs Study*, Paris.

OECD, 2014, 'How Is Life in Greece', OECD Better Life Initiative, retrieved from http://www.oecd.org/statistics/BLI%202014%20Greece%20country%20report.pdf.

Politaki, A., 2013, 'Greece is Facing a Humanitarian Crisis,' *The Guardian*, 11 February, retrieved from http://www.theguardian.com/commentisfree/2013/feb/11/greece-humanitarian-crisis-eu.

Potthoff, H., 1965, *Die Montanunion in der Europäischen Gemeinschaft: Eine Zwischenbilanz*, Hannover: Verlag für Literatur und Zeitgeschehen.

Rieger, E., 1996, 'Agrarpolitik: Integration durch Gemeinschaftspolitik?', in Jachtenfuchs, M. and Kohler-Koch, B., eds., *Europäische Integration*, Opladen: Leske & Budrich Verlag.

Rogoff, K., 1996, 'The Purchasing Power Parity Puzzle', *Journal of Economic Literature* XXXIV, June: 647–668.

Ros, J., 2000, *Development Theory and the Economics of Growth*. Ann Arbor, MI: University of Michigan Press.

Schäuble, W., 2011, 'Why Austerity Is the Only Cure for the Eurozone', *Financial Times*, 5 September.

Schumpeter, J.A., 1912, *Theorie der wirtschaftlichen Entwicklung*, Leipzig: Duncker & Humblot.

Schumpeter, J.A., 1954, *History of Economic Analysis*, Oxford: Oxford University Press.

Thiel, E., 1998, *Die Europäische Union: Von der Integration der Märkte zu gemeinsamen Politiken*, Opladen: Leske & Budrich Verlag.

UNCTAD, *Trade and Development Report*, New York and Geneva: United Nations.

UNICEF, 2014, 'Report. The Condition of Chilren in Greece', Greek National Committee, Athens, retrieved from http://www.unicef.gr/uploads/filemanager/PDF/2014/children-in-greece-2014.pdf.